A Bouquet *of* Roses

# A Bouquet of Roses

### GLORIOUS ARRANGEMENTS FOR ALL OCCASIONS

BY **CHRISTINA WRESSELL**

TEXT BY **KATE CHYNOWETH**

PHOTOGRAPHS BY **SUSIE CUSHNER**

**CHRONICLE BOOKS**

SAN FRANCISCO

Library of Congress Cataloging-in-Publication Data available.

ISBN 0-8118-4108-1

MANUFACTURED IN Hong Kong

FLORAL DESIGN BY Christina Wressell
DESIGNED BY Alissar Rayes

DISTRIBUTED IN CANADA BY
Raincoast Books
9050 Shaughnessy Street
Vancouver, British Columbia V6P 6E5

10 9 8 7 6 5 4 3 2 1

CHRONICLE BOOKS LLC
85 Second Street
San Francisco, California 94105

www.chroniclebooks.com

A C K N O W L E D G M E N T S

∽

The first attraction to working with flowers was that it offered an outlet for thought and feeling using color—for me, a revelation. I was able to articulate a sensation or mood in my mind and make it tangible.

I am grateful to Rick Urban and Ellen Readio for hiring me and allowing me to merge the idea of flower shop and science lab. I met Rick when I was 17 and Ellen when I was 20, and both gave me the opportunity to explore flowers without holding me to such high standards that I was discouraged. When I was 24, I moved to Aspen and was blessed with meeting Beth Gill, a mentor and important friend for life. I learned that flowers are not just about creating a pretty thing to look at, there are many facets of the business that need to be learned and honed as each day presents itself.

In New York, I wouldn't have a world like I have now without Patti Wilson and Eric Berthold. They opened a door to styling photographs that was vital in creating this book. I am so lucky and indebted to both for their prodding and teaching and guidance and friendship. And Mari Faucher, my agent, for all of your countless hours, patience, counsel, and confidence. I would not have been able to have done any of this without you.

Hilarity in life allows me to get through the tough times and makes the fun times even better. I can't imagine a life without it. I love and thank those friends with whom I laugh, joke, and sometimes cry, and who have supported me through this endeavor. Amie Murstein, Angèle Parlange, Huit Hertzog, and Melanie Acevedo—you all are a source of support and inspiration when you don't even know it.

Susie, Josh, and Scott, my family, who light up my life. You are wise and unfettered humans. Thank you for being so. And to the Cochon, the sweetest boy of all, who is my everything.

Leslie Jonath, of Chronicle Books, gave me an opportunity to author this book and I thank her a million times over. I have learned much in the process and, most importantly, that it is a process. Kate Chynoweth for her endless words and tireless phone calls and p-a-t-i-e-n-c-e. And, finally, Susie Cushner for beautiful pictures and spirit.

# TABLE *of* CONTENTS

When George Bernard Shaw declared his belief "in the might of design, in the mystery of color, the redemption of all things by Beauty everlasting," he was writing of masterpiece paintings, but such words are equally appropriate praise for the rose. Roses, more than any other flower, capture the essence of color.

There are lavender roses that remind me of rainy summer skies, and lush apricot blooms that evoke a brilliant sunset. From luscious yellow and cream to vivid pink, from deep crimson to orange and gold, there is a rose to fit every mood. In Victorian England, where yellow roses stood for jealousy and white signified trust, rose color spoke a complex language all its own. In my eighteen years as a florist, I've discovered my own color vocabulary—how to use flowers to create texture, contrast, and harmony, and to capture mood and ambience.

I hope that the colorful arrangements in these pages will inspire you to discover your own sense of color, using both roses and the many other gorgeous flowers that work so beautifully with them.

*Flora Domestica*, a wonderful book on the history of British flower arranging, describes how 1930s hostesses harmonized flower arrangements with the colors of walls and furnishings in their homes—and how guests followed suit by coordinating their outfits with their hostesses' decor. "Such was the attention to detail at this time that it was not unusual for ladies to ascertain the color of the rooms in their host's house in order to wear both dresses and flowers that would complement them," the author writes. In today's more casual world, few of us consider such details. However, to me, color is still of reigning importance when it comes to flower arranging.

As *A Bouquet of Roses* came together, it seemed most natural to organize it by color. Not only does color inspire me, but I find it's also the best way to articulate a feeling or an occasion's very essence. White embodies a simple, fresh elegance, while deep red feels more formal, perfectly capturing the spirit of the holidays or a grand celebration. Ethereal pink speaks volumes of romance. For me, there's also a practical reason for selecting a color first, since most flower markets and shops group their roses by hue, with pinks together, reds together, and so forth. Knowing the color I'm after saves time and helps me focus, since I can go straight to it and then decide on shape and texture rather than getting distracted by the many color options.

Color relates to nearly each choice you make regarding your arrangement, such as its placement in your home. Lighting and background are also important to consider. Pale, creamy roses glow in dim light, while a bouquet of deep red roses can disappear in a shadowy corner. Conversely, dark colors do well against pale backgrounds. Color is also an important consideration when you are choosing your container, which should enhance rather than compete with your flowers (see Containers, page 19).

Beginners shouldn't necessarily start by choosing neutral colors. I learned to embrace color by paying attention to what draws the eye. For instance, I've always liked the combination of pink and green (see page 63). I joke that this is the result of my preppy upbringing, but the more scientific explanation is that pink and green are complementary colors. (On a color wheel, green is the complement of red; since pink is simply a tint of red, it makes sense that these colors enhance each other.) Traditional color science does indeed provide guidance and, although the rules can be found in most basic style books (see Bibliography for details), my favorite approach is to just start throwing colors together and see what makes me fall in love. One of my favorite contrasts is that of lavender and terra-cotta roses, a combination I stumbled across while creating the Kissing Ball (page 125). On the other hand, the subtle contrasts in a monochromatic scheme also have immense appeal, and making this type of arrangement is easy for beginners (although I still make them all the time). These combine tints and shades of a single color, as with Mauve Mix (page 118). Using a monochromatic scheme makes choosing the colors for your arrangement incredibly easy, and the results are always gorgeous.

Since color is everywhere, we can easily become overwhelmed by the many hues, shades and variations that are available. That is why it's important to collect and file away the concepts that strike you. Fabrics can be a source of inspiration. The saturated color and lush petals of red 'Traviata' garden roses reminded me of rich, textured velvet. If you have a favorite piece of upholstered furniture, you can mimic its color simply by holding up color swatches next to an array of flowers of different colors until you find the right one. With roses, there are so many colors that it's a cinch to find a good match. When I travel outside of New York, retail stores are my favorite haunts; checking out the shop displays from Paris to San Francisco always yields fresh ideas, and the seasons are always a muse. Spring twilight might inspire a loose display of soft lavender roses, while a field of summer wildflowers and Queen Anne's lace might call for a country arrangement.

When it comes to color, the best rule of thumb is to see what draws your attention. I encourage you to experiment and let your own sensibility guide you. Ultimately, the choice of color illustrates a specific kind of style, and each person has his or her own.

## CHOOSING ROSES

Modern roses have a rich, ancient heritage that stretches deep into the past. In fact, fossil evidence suggests that wild roses existed as far back as 32 million years ago. The details of these early species are lost to time, but we do know that roses flourished long before people tended to them in flower gardens or even walked the earth. Experts agree that cultivation began in China, approximately 5,000 years ago, and that ancient roses grew around the globe, in Asia, Europe, and the New World.

The debut of the rose as we know it today came with the arrival of the flowers classified as antique roses. The roses in this class, such as Gallica, Damask, and Alba—types that ultimately played an important role in the parentage of modern English roses—were established by the end of the eighteenth century. Perfumed with a rich, true rose scent and graced with full, rosette-shaped flowers, these blooms range in color from deep pink to purple and from pale pink to white. Surprisingly, true crimson and soft yellow, colors that are considered classic for roses today, are seen only in modern hybrid varieties that took root during the nineteenth century. The impetus for these new roses came with the China rose—a repeat bloomer, unlike other varieties at the time—which appeared in Europe in 1799. Hybridizations of the China rose yielded five new families of roses: Chinas, Portlands, Bourbons, Hybrid Perpetuals, and Teas. These new rose families paved the way for the development in 1867 of modern roses such as Hybrid Teas, Floribundas, Grandifloras, Miniatures, and English roses, all of which come in a multiplicity of colors. With more than 12,000 varieties of roses available today, it's helpful to know these basic classifications, so that you can distinguish one rose from another. However, when it comes to arranging, your eye for color and shape will eventually create an internal list that is even more helpful to you.

Between June and October, most of my rose arrangements are made with garden roses from California. These lush, perfumed, vividly colored blossoms are as breathtaking in elaborate bridal bouquets as they are in simple table adornments. Unless you grow them yourself in the garden, these roses must generally be special ordered. However, I also rely on hothouse roses from South America, the type available in local floral shops. These colorful roses can be purchased in flower markets and shops in major cities throughout the year. I'm a great fan of these flowers. They come in a dazzling array of gorgeous colors, and their only real drawback is their faint scent (although some varieties do boast more of a scent than others).

Of the hothouse varieties that are commonly found in shops, I'm always drawn to the 'Leonidas' rose, a beautiful earthy blossom that ranges from cinnamon orange to a striking, almost terra-cotta color. If I'm after lavender, I seek out 'Blue Curiosa' roses, for their elegant shape. Another good lavender rose is 'Sterling', because it tends to have more of a true rose fragrance than most shop varieties. Among the red roses, a dramatic favorite of mine is the 'Black Beauty' rose. With its dark blooms and crimson-edged petals, this blossom instantly creates a sexy mood.

When I arrive at the flower market or shop, I search out what looks fresh and hardy. When you are purchasing roses on your own, here are some additional helpful hints to consider:

✐ Look for hardy roses that are open just a little bit; don't purchase a rose that is fully open. Gently touch the blossoms, to see if they feel silky and firm. Avoid weak roses, for example those whose buttery, soft outer petals fall off at the gentlest touch.

✐ Garden roses are shown in many of the arrangements in this book, but if they're not easily accessible in your area, simply find an approximate color substitute. If an arrangement in these pages features a red garden rose, buy a rose in the closest hue of red you can find in a shop. The blooms won't be quite as lush, and the fragrance won't be as intense, but your arrangement will still have the rich, saturated color and elegance of the original depicted herein.

✐ If your heart is set on garden roses, be sure to plan in advance. (I source garden roses directly from a grower in Santa Barbara called Rose Hill Gardens, www.rhg.com.) Some florists may be able to place a special order for you, but usually only if they have an established relationship with a garden rose grower. The extended season for garden roses is from the end of March to the end of October; these roses are most easily accessible between June and September.

✐ Some roses have more perfume than others, so if scent is a major consideration, choose your rose type carefully. Garden roses tend to emit a strong and memorable perfume, whereas hothouse roses tend to vary, from having a slight fragrance to having almost none. If you make a bridal bouquet, for example, an old-fashioned rose scent is important and it's worth the effort to seek out lushly aromatic garden roses such as David Austin's 'Gertrude Jekyll'. With other arrangements, such as a cheerful bouquet in a hallway or entry, it's perfectly fine to use roses that may lack much perfume but bring a profusion of color.

## ROSE RECOMMENDATIONS BY COLOR

Roses today come in a dizzying number of colors, and even previously rare shades such as pale green and true apricot are readily available. I enjoy working with all types of roses, including the lush, many-petaled English roses, but by far the most common roses in my arrangements are modern Hybrid Teas. These are the types of roses that can be found in shops year-round and are the most accessible to the home arranger. They tend to have long, elegant, pointed buds that open to pretty blossoms with high centers and reflexed outer petals that curve down. Hybrid Teas are essentially "double roses," meaning they carry 17 to 25 petals; their ability to bloom throughout the year and resist disease has led to an explosion in growth and hybridization of Hybrid Teas. As a result, this variety boasts a wider array of colors than any other type of rose. Unfortunately, not all the Hybrid Tea roses are created equal, and some come in colors that are garish or "hot" compared with other varieties, making them less desirable when you're trying to create color harmony in arrangements. Experimentation with different types will lead you to discover certain favorites; read on for a list of some of my own.

Not all the recommendations below are Hybrid Tea roses, however. Some even fall into the category of the English rose, which tends to be generously sized and have an abundant look that is easily distinguishable from the Hybrid Teas. The blooms are generally more complex, whorled, and varied in appearance than modern Hybrid Tea roses (which despite their elegance can look monotonous if used too much). Many of the roses are usually either "full" (having 26 to 40 petals) or "very full" (having 41 petals or more). English roses were first introduced in the 1950s by David Austin, a British hybridizer who successfully combined modern Floribundas and Hybrid Teas with two of the oldest types of roses, Gallicas and Damasks to create a whole new breed of rose. Austin's English roses are among my favorites for arranging because of their exquisite "old rose" characteristics, such as a gorgeous fragrance, many-petaled blooms, and rich, saturated colors that seem to glow from within. Some of his varieties set whole new standards for lushness; the 'Pilgrim' rose, for example, carries a luxuriant 170 petals on each bloom. While the color spectrum of garden roses is more limited than that of Hybrid Teas (for example, there is no pale-green English rose), their natural beauty and form is unparalleled. These roses are generally available only through special order from your own cutting garden, but they are well worth seeking out. If you are creating one of the arrangements in this book and cannot find a particular garden rose, substitute a Hybrid Tea rose with similar characteristics and color.

White roses
'Akito'
'Avalanche'
'Bianca'
'Honor'
'Iceberg'
'Fair Bianca'
'Mistique'
'Snowball'
'Vendela'

Red roses
'Black Beauty'
'Classy'
'Enigma'
'Estelle'
'Isabel Renaissance'
'L. D. Braithwaite'
'Olympiad'
'Preference'
'Traviata'

True pink roses
'Auguste Renoir'
'Gertrude Jekyll'
'Guy de Maupassant'
'Hot Princess'
'Latin Ambience'
'Tiffany'
'Yves Piaget'

Apricot, orange, or warm-blend roses
'Abraham Darby'
'Brandy'
'Evelyn'
'Just Joey'
'King's Pride'
'Leonidas'
'Mirable'
'Macarena'
'Perdita'
'Rio Samba'
'Sunset Celebration'
'Touch of Class'

Yellow roses
'Dakar'
'Golden Celebration'
'Gina Lollobrigida'
'Graham Thomas'
'Jenny'
'Jean Giono'
'Skyline'
'Saint Patrick'
'Toulouse Lautrec'
'Yellow Island'

Lavender or mauve roses
'Blue Curiosa'
'Heirloom'
'Paradise'
'Paul Neyron'
'Stainless Steel'

Pale pink roses
'Anna'
'Bewitched'
'Ilse'
'Paris de Yves St. Laurent'
'Secret'

The following are some other hues that I use less frequently.

Green roses
'Jade'
'Limon'
'Super Green'

Multicolored roses
'Brigadoon' (pink and cream)
'Oranges 'n' Lemons' (orange and yellow)

## PREPARING AND CONDITIONING

Even when flowers are very fresh, as you might find when buying them direct from a wholesale flower market in a major city like San Francisco or New York, I recommend putting them in water as soon as possible (wait absolutely no longer than 4 hours). Store them in room-temperature water and don't refrigerate them. Putting the roses in very cold water will shock them, and they will fail to open up.

In my experience, the key to long-lasting roses is to use a very clean container—not just the vase, but any vessel that holds the flowers at any point. I often store the flowers I've purchased in clean buckets of room-temperature water until I'm ready to use them. Before placing the roses in the buckets or vases, I wash the containers out with a bleach-and-water mixture and a stiff brush. This ensures that the vessels are free of bacteria, which can harm roses and cause them to wither. You can submerge the roses in a bucket, including the leaves, as long as the rose blooms remain above the water.

When it comes to conditioning roses, I do it the natural way—just with water—and without any tricks. However, many of my arrangements are not meant to last for more than one or two nights. So if you're really hoping to prolong the life of an arrangement, take the advice of rose expert Ray Reddell: add 1 teaspoon of sugar and a few drops of household bleach to 1 quart of hot water and use that in your vase. You can also experiment with the preservatives available from floral shops, always keeping in mind that starting with a clean container—and not shocking the roses with cold water—is absolutely crucial.

Before making any rose arrangement, it's essential to strip most of the leaves and the thorns from the stem. Approach this potentially painful task with attention and care, making sure to protect your hands and use the appropriate tools. Wear gloves, preferably cotton or canvas ones with additional leather on the palm (these can be found at garden stores or hardware stores). Rose thorns are best stripped with a tool called a "rose stripper," available at garden shops and some hardware stores. If you find yourself without gloves or tools, don't attempt to flick off the thorns with a knife; instead, you may carefully attempt the emergency method of bunching up a cotton or linen dish towel (don't use terry cloth—it's too porous) and dragging it down the stem, removing thorns as you go. However, this approach will not work for very thorny roses and it's no substitute for using the correct tools.

17

When it's time to make your arrangement, always take care not to clip the stems too short; you can always cut them again, but you can't replace a stem that has been cut. When in doubt, measure the stems against the container before cutting them.

Before moving the roses from the bucket into the final container, I recut the stems while the flowers remain submerged in water. Cutting the rose under water prevents the stem from drawing air (this helps combat the problem of drooping heads). Also, the moisture puts a natural sealant on the stem that protects it as you transfer the flowers between vessels. You can also prolong the loveliness of an arrangement with aftercare, for instance recutting the stems (clipping about $\frac{1}{4}$ inch to $\frac{1}{2}$ inch of the stem each time) under running water about every other day.

## CUTTING FROM THE GARDEN

If you are cutting roses from the garden, it's ideal to make the cuts in the early morning or late afternoon, since this is when the blossoms retain the most moisture. Some rosarians suggest cutting only the flower buds that are no more than half open. However, deciding at which stage to cut a bloom is more of an art than a science. Experimentation is truly the best teacher. Some varieties will open nicely from a half-open bud while others, particularly those with many-petaled blossoms, such as some modern varieties, will only be truly magnificent in the vase if they first develop fully on the bush. When you cut, be sure that the portion of stem you leave behind has at least two sets of leaves (each set generally has five or more leaflets). Cutting too long a stem may weaken your plants. Make the cut just above a leaf, to encourage a new stem to grow.

*A Bouquet of Roses*

## CONTAINERS

From the bright whimsy of a vintage teapot to the heavy elegance of a silver urn, containers often provoke as much enthusiasm as do the flowers inside them. I'm an equal-opportunity employer when it comes to containers. I adore antiques and always keep at least one really pretty etched-glass piece or ironstone pitcher on hand, but I frequently turn the house inside out to find just the right old cup or bowl. A rummage through an antique store or a garden shop can also yield some treasures. Here are a few simple tips on containers:

Raid the kitchen. Plastic liners can help you transform unexpected items into wonderful containers. A lovely old wooden bowl has great appeal, and using a liner (the type of plastic tray you put beneath your potted plants) makes it a viable container. The same technique works with silver or pewter bowls, which are easy to find in almost any antique shop or flea market and make for beautiful arrangements. You can even use a Pyrex glass bowl. If you search with an eye toward shape, you'll make plenty of unexpected finds around the house.

Keep it simple. At local garden centers or good hardware stores, you can always find terra-cotta pots. One easy way to give them some personality is to spray paint the pots different colors; I always buy several and paint at least a couple of them white—they're endlessly useful. You can put a plastic liner over the hole at the bottom of the pot and make the arrangement inside or, depending on the size of the pot, place a cup inside and place the flowers there.

Experiment with shape. Whether it's a rustic square planter, a tall bamboo cylinder, or a galvanized tin bucket, every shape can bring delight to the eye. Bowls are also ideal containers, because they are wide enough to hold the flowers without the use of wire or tricks; their shape is especially suited to my arrangements, which tend to be round and densely packed. But don't bypass the more unusual shapes. I have a lovely fan-shaped ceramic vase; peach roses look terrific against its rich brown glaze, and the unique shape gives the arrangement visual interest.

Use your local resources. High-end flower shops can be a good place to find containers, and most can special order what you need if they don't usually stock it. I never settle for the standard "ginger jar" florist vase when I can have a tall cylinder or a glass bubble, which I find more appealing. Even at small establishments, specific requests are often met. The more detail you provide, the better; for example, you might ask for a short, wide, frosted-glass cylinder rather than just a cylinder. (I prefer frosted glass over clear. It hides the flower stems, drawing more attention to the blooms themselves.)

Go beyond glass. I always keep some glass on hand, but I'm equally drawn to other types of materials. I love ceramic containers because their glazes offer so much variety. Iridescent glazes, for example, can work with an array of colors—a pearly white with hints of pale green, lavender, and pink is a perfect foil for yellow or orange roses. Wooden containers also offer an incredible range of color, from aged pine to dark oak or walnut. Pairing light-colored roses with a dark-hued container, such as pale pink roses in a mahogany vessel, always yields gorgeous results.

## A FEW NOTES ON TECHNIQUE

Creating a sturdy base to anchor your flowers is essential to a balanced arrangement. For small, round, densely packed arrangements, using a voluminous base flower, such as hydrangea, is usually enough to hold the other flowers in place. With larger displays that require more control, I usually opt for chicken wire. It's a cinch to roll the wire into a ball, place the ball inside your chosen container, and then drop the flowers in. A "frog," a pronged florist's tool that holds stems in place, is another option. Easily found at most flower shops and hardware stores, this tool comes in many sizes and provides an anchor for your stems. Both options work best with flowers that have thicker stems; for thin-stemmed varieties, try Oasis.

Oasis is water-absorbent foam that forms an excellent base for arrangements. If you feel uncertain about how to make an arrangement or how to hold one together—or if you find that the flowers easily fall out of their container—working with Oasis is a good solution. My technique is to fully submerge a block of Oasis in water for about 10 minutes. Once it has absorbed the liquid, you can shape it with your fingers, put it into your bowl, and voilà! It works like putty to hold the stems in place. Due to its high chemical content, it's advisable to wash your hands after handling Oasis.

20

If you are tying bouquets, search out wired ribbon. It's easy to work with because it has more structure than regular ribbon and is readily available in card or gift stores by the yard. The wire is generally very fine and not noticeable until you bend it. When using wired ribbon to hold a bouquet together, have someone else hold the bouquet, and wrap the ribbon around the stems in a crisscross pattern down the length of the stems. (For further details, see the Gothic Jewel arrangement, page 38.)

When you're making a tall, heavy arrangement such as a large centerpiece or entryway bouquet, always plan to make the arrangement on site; in other words, carry the vase to its final location, along with all the flowers, and do your work there. (I generally fill the vase just halfway with water until the display is completed, in order to prevent spills while I'm working.) Bring a watering can to fill the container fully when the arrangement is completed. If you make the display off site and then move it to its destination, the flowers you've worked so hard to balance can get all jumbled and out of whack as you carry them.

Even when you are in a rush, it's important to pause and think about every step before you dive into making your bouquet; this will prevent miscalculations and ensure the flowers end up looking just as you planned.

ARRANGEMENTS *by* COLOR

25

45

67

85

101

115

Red

# Red

- *Purple anemone*
- *'Enigma' roses*

## FESTIVE RED TABLE

Beautiful roses are simply too good to keep to oneself, which is the main reason we display them around the house or invite friends to visit our rose garden in bloom. You can go one step further by providing your guests with their very own bouquet of roses, putting one at each place setting. Guests can then carry a memento of the festive evening from your home into their own.

'Enigma' roses and purple anemone set at each guest's place setting prove that large arrangements are not the only way to create an impact with flowers. This very simple approach involves placing the flowers in a small glass on the top plate of each table setting. The flower stems are cut fairly short and the ratio of flowers is approximately 2 or 3 anemones to 4 roses per glass. I tend to cluster each type of flower together—roses with roses, anemones with anemones—to maximize the color and shape impact of the blossoms. Since the roses are the stars of the table, it's essential to give them plenty of time to open so the cupped blossoms are at their fullest. To be safe, I'd buy the roses 2 days prior to the party, hydrate them well, and leave them at room temperature. (Even though you often see refrigerated flowers in shops, you should never

refrigerate them yourself. Certain foods in your refrigerator, such as apples, can react with the roses and cause the petals to wilt.) In the festive candlelight of a dinner party, the deep-red roses glow with inviting warmth.

Red 'Enigma' is grown in hothouses and should be available throughout the year, but if you have trouble finding it, other red varieties such as 'Classy' would work equally well. The scarlet color scheme of this table is especially well suited to winter celebrations, from a holiday dinner party to a cozy gathering on a chilly winter evening. Using the table linens and dishes to pick up the flowers' color enhances the overall effect. Here, I displayed red glass and, rather than buying a tablecloth, used a piece of plum-colored cotton velvet; the matte texture is more elegant than the shiny look of other types of

28

velvet, such as silk velvets or blends. If you're using place cards, you can nestle a place card in the bouquet or lean one against the vase. The concept translates well to any season; in spring, for instance, you might pair sunny yellow roses with white hyacinths or white tulips.

A good way to maximize the effect of simple arrangements is to employ layered lighting, as shown here. For example, the votive candles provide low lighting, while an overhead chandelier and unusual iron candelabra provide illumination from above. The colored glass is a nice touch that helps bring the look together. What I've used here are actually pretty red cocktail glasses; upscale home stores are a good place to find something along these lines. Antique versions are often more expensive but bring beautiful results. I usually seek out opaque glasses to hide the stems, but because there are only a few flowers in each of these bouquets, the stems don't create too much of a distraction. If you were doing larger bouquets, however, or using flowers with thick woody stems, an alabaster or opaque container would be the best choice. You can be as whimsical as you like at your own dinner party; to create a quaint mood, you could place vintage teacups filled with flowers at each setting. For a very formal occasion, you could create a large centerpiece out of the same flowers, and the flower-filled glasses would then act as gorgeous satellite bouquets.

29

- *Evergreen garland*
- *'Black Beauty' roses*
- *Cranberry ribbon*

## GORGEOUS GARLAND

We could probably survive the holidays without decorating with combinations of red and green, but why would we want to? These colors are as essential to the season as the chilly temperatures of winter itself. My ideal party decoration for this time of year is not the ubiquitous poinsettias that dominate the shop fronts, but a stunning garland of greenery laced with vibrant red roses. It hits just the right note at an elegant party.

The holidays are a busy time for most of us, and if you're planning to host a Yuletide celebration, undertaking a massive floral project is probably the first item on your not-to-do list. But this display is actually much easier than it appears, if you special order the garland and add the finishing touch—the roses—yourself. 'Black Beauty' roses are a favorite of mine for this display because their color is deeper and more voluptuous than the typical bright holiday red; the blossoms have a rich cranberry hue that truly resonates against the greenery. Other fine substitutes include 'Black Baccara' and 'Black Magic' roses.

Red roses transform the garland into a cheerful holiday ornament, but you can use other colors of rose if you prefer. An alternative color scheme that is especially fresh and beautiful for the holidays is a combination of green and white; if you take this approach, white roses such as 'Avalanche' or 'Akito' roses, which are available throughout the year, are good choices.

When you're choosing the ribbon to weave through the garland, it's a good idea to match it to the flowers (the cranberry color of the French ribbon shown here is almost an exact match to that of the 'Black Beauty' roses). Silver offsets the deep shades in the garland beautifully, so I like to complete the look with some festive silver ornaments, candlesticks, or—my personal favorite—mercury-glass vases like those displayed on the mantelpiece. Magnolia garlands like the one shown here are traditional mainly in the South and finding them elsewhere in the country can

31

be a bit of a challenge. Evergreen garlands are excellent substitutes and cost much less. I've had great success working with Douglas fir, cedar, and green spruce, but I recommend against using pine. Bay leaf and olive leaf garlands are beautiful as well. Whatever greenery you use, this garland doesn't have great lasting power, and it's not something to leave up all through the holidays; rather, it's as festive and ephemeral as the evening itself.

Garlands can usually be ordered from your florist or local garden center, and the standard size—8 to 12—should suffice unless you have a very large mantel. First, secure the garland in place on the mantel: "hide" 4 nails on the underside of the mantel; then loop 18-gauge floral wire around the garland, attaching each end of the loop of wire (which will hold up the garland) to a single nail. Next, weave the colored ribbon through the garland, working with the garland to create depth and dimension. (If you decide to light the garland, turn on the lights before you start.) I usually cut the ribbon into 3 sections so I can finish the 2 opposing ends in a special way (see style of cut as shown in photo, page 31) to create pretty dangling ribbon ends along each side. Where I want the ribbon to stay put in the garland, I stuff it in deeply using a pencil or other pointy object. Usually just cramming the ribbon into the crevice will do the trick. Finally, to incorporate the 'Black Beauty' roses, put them in pointed water tubes, sometimes called water picks, so they stay fresh, and then stick the tubes in amid the greenery and ribbon. The tubes, which have rubber stoppers with a hole in the top and a point at the bottom, can be found at floral shops. The first step is to cut the rose stems to the size of the tubes and insert the ends into the water-filled reservoir. It's easy to attach the tubes to the garland because each tube is pointed on its end. Use the previously placed ribbon as a guide for where to put the roses.

- *'Classy' roses*
- *'L. D. Braithwaite' roses*
- *'Secret' roses*

## LOVER'S BREAKFAST

Whether the occasion is Valentine's Day or an anniversary celebration, this easy arrangement creates a wonderful ambience. The rich, dark-red hues whisper of romance while the 'L. D. Braithwaite', a sumptuous David Austin rose, intoxicates with its true rose scent. What better way to wake up on a special morning? Add piping-hot coffee and fresh pastries and you and your sweetheart might just linger over breakfast all day.

Roses are red, as the saying goes. Ironically, however, it can be difficult to find the perfect crimson flower. Reds tend to fade more quickly than other colors, sometimes to shades that are less than desirable. Fortunately, there are some red roses you can count on, such as the 'L. D. Braithwaite', which opens remarkably wide to a beautiful, loose-petaled bloom and has a strong, true rose fragrance. It is among the brightest crimson of the English roses, and the color lasts beautifully. (David Austin, who describes this flower as embodying the best characteristics of both of its rose parents, named this rose after his father-in-law.) 'Classy', the other red rose shown, is a hothouse variety available throughout the year. While the hue of 'Classy' doesn't have the incredible saturation or staying power of 'L. D. Braithwaite', it's a wonderful (and less

expensive) base for the arrangement. The cream-colored 'Secret', a modern Hybrid Tea garden rose, lightens the bouquet and brings the colors together. Its blooms provide contrast while the pink-edged petals echo the red of the other roses. The shapes of the roses in this arrangement are a study in contrasting forms. The wide, loose-petaled bloom of the 'L. D. Braithwaite', which more closely resembles an "old rose" formation, is easy to differentiate from the more elongated heads of roses such as 'Classy' or 'Secret'.

A modern, cream-colored tea service such as this one is invaluable for versatile table arrangements. Coffee cups, creamers, and sugar bowls all provide ample room for flowers, and are charming as vessels. They are perfect for series arrangements, as you can easily place

33

the main bouquet in a medium-sized pottery piece and the satellites in smaller pieces, letting the uniformity of the glaze bring the look together. For this arrangement, I chose the teapot as a vessel because it has ample room to contain the stems (so there was no need for Oasis or wire). Most of the bouquet comprises the 'Classy' roses and they create enough volume to make it easy to just fill in a few specialty roses in addition. (In general, the flower I'm using to create maximum volume is often referred to as the "base" flower of an arrangement.) I added the deep crimson 'L. D. Braithwaite' garden roses, making sure to give them front-and-center placement to highlight their full, dramatic shape and incredible crimson color. I finished by adding the cream-colored roses, which help to create a frame of sorts around the red roses. Make sure that the heads are distributed evenly for weight to prevent the arrangement from looking unbalanced.

*A Bouquet of Roses*

- *'Black Baccara' roses*
- *Black calla lilies*
- *Chocolate cosmos*

# BLACK BEAUTY

The blackest night can seem to pulse with sensuous, velvety colors, and so in this arrangement the flowers are suffused with deep yet vibrant hues. The striking black calla lilies tend toward magenta, a rich purplish red, while the chocolate cosmos reside at the darkest end of the color spectrum. It's wonderfully unexpected to combine classic red roses, traditionally displayed on their own, with these unusually shaped and textured flowers.

An autumn dinner party instantly becomes more elegant when you decorate the buffet with dark, velvety flowers set in a beautiful container of mercury glass. I came across this particular vase in an antique store and fell in love with its old-fashioned charm. The reflective silver provides a stunning contrast with the 'Black Baccara' roses, which have a seductive dark-crimson color and open nicely from elegantly pointed buds into cupped blossoms. If possible, buy the roses only if they are more than halfway open, since that will make it easier to coax them into full opening. When you get them home, place them in a warm spot in the house in a vase of tepid water.

These roses are available throughout the year, but if you can't find them, good substitutes include 'Black Beauty' or 'Black Magic' roses.

Calla lilies can be readily found in fall and winter, although this color is rare in shops and may need to be special ordered. The crisp, fluted form of the callas adds an interesting three-dimensional component to the display; here, I used smaller specimens since the larger variety would have overwhelmed the other components. The chocolate cosmos, used in this arrangement for texture and size contrast, are available throughout the fall. They're one of my favorite elements to use in autumn displays for their tiny, velvety petals and lovely dark centers, which have an almost beaded appearance. Their heavenly scent really does smell like chocolate! Cosmos also come in many other colors, including rose, pink, magenta, lavender, and white; blooms in these colors generally have sunny yellow centers.

How you make this arrangement will depend on the sort of vessel you use. The silver bowl shown here was a bit too shallow to contain all the stems without help, so I used Oasis, a floral foam, to anchor the stems. If you use a larger, deeper bowl, or even a silver pitcher, you could probably get away with just using water. If you do use Oasis, the first step is to soak it in water for approximately 10 minutes. Once it becomes quite heavy and can be easily manipulated, mash it up into small, pebblelike pieces with your fingers. Place the mass of Oasis at the bottom of the bowl and fill the container halfway with water. When the Oasis is in place, all that remains is to insert the flowers stem by stem, starting with the roses, then adding the callas, and finishing with the cosmos. It's best to group a number of calla lilies, chocolate cosmos, and roses together so each component of the display is striking and visible. The beauty of working with Oasis is that it's easy to correct any mistakes in form by changing the flowers' positions. Once you've reached a basic form that pleases you, rotate the bowl 45 degrees and add final touches of cosmos or fill in with the other flowers where you spot gaps or spaces, always being sure that a few blooms gracefully camouflage the rim of the container.

- *'Traviata' roses*
- *'Blue Curiosa' roses*
- *Red scabiosa*
- *Red velvet ribbon*

## Gothic Jewel

Gothic romance, with all its sensational, melancholy, and supernatural qualities, is embodied in this arrangement of rich red and dark burgundy flowers, lightened with a touch of lavender. Bursting from a narrow-necked black vase, these tightly gathered blossoms demand attention. The arrangement shape provides a wonderful showcase for the dark red 'Traviata' garden rose, which has about 100 petals tucked into each exquisite bloom. To enhance the moodiness and romantic effect, you can create several arrangements for a series effect.

Tied like a handheld bouquet and secured with red velvet ribbon, this dark, romantic arrangement features colors that simply glow against a light background. The shape is refreshing for a tabletop adornment and looks beautiful on a buffet, or on a side table in the living room (preferably next to a lamp that is slightly higher than the arrangement so the lighting enhances the effect). Ribbon-tied bouquets are very popular at weddings, but in the right container this classic shape is incredibly versatile. The style provides a wonderful showcase for one of my favorite red garden roses, 'Traviata'. This Romantica Hybrid Tea is relatively new, dating to 1998, but it has quickly become popular for its saturated, dark red hue. The fragrance is quite light. But whether you use this particular rose or a hothouse variety such as 'Black Beauty', the key is to lighten the overall dark effect with a few pale, glimmering blossoms. Here, lavender 'Blue Curiosa' roses do the trick, although 'Anna', a pale pink rose that is usually easy to order from a florist, would also provide the necessary contrast. A touch of crimson velvet ribbon enhances the arrangement's gothic appeal and provides a welcome bit of texture. The rich-colored blossoms truly resonate in this black opaque glass vase. If you are having trouble finding a vessel in this rather unusual shape, explore antique shops and flea markets; those shown here are from The End of History, a wonderful shop in Manhattan that accepts telephone orders and offers a wide array of vintage and modern containers in beautiful colored glass.

Composing this bouquet couldn't be easier. It's as simple as cutting all the stems to the same length—keeping them long enough to hit water in a tall vase—and wrapping them with velvet ribbon. To begin, I take hold of the larger roses first and then fill the bouquet in with scabiosa, holding it steady in my hand. It's helpful to insert the scabiosa through the top and pull the bottom of each stem down with your free hand (always being careful not to pop off the heads of the scabiosa). To finish, I wrap the stems with the ribbon from the top down.

Placing 2 similar arrangements in close proximity enhances their effect and, in this case, shows off the diverse, unique shapes of the vases available in this striking colored glass. Another option is to seek out 4 or 5 smaller glass vases and create a series of small hand-tied bouquets; the idea behind "series" arrangements is to create a voluminous look without having to construct a huge floral display. You can even create a shape with the small vases, arranging them in a circle, for example, in the center of a coffee table or dining room table.

## Tea and Sympathy

When a friend needs a little cheering up, this simple, easily portable arrangement of roses is the perfect solution. Of course, you needn't wait for a social occasion to break out this easy and affordable bouquet; it's a wonderful visual pick-me-up, and you'll enjoy the sight of the gorgeous flowers as much as you will seeing your favorite tea set on the table.

When you only have time to do the minimum, monochromatic arrangements can't be beat. They can be completed in minutes, and always look beautiful. Choosing which rose to use is particularly important when just one type will take the spotlight. In summer, romantica garden roses are my favorites, because of their deep-cupped, many-petaled blossoms. A small, low arrangement such as this Asian teacup packed with flowers is just about the most versatile form of bouquet. It will look especially charming on the kitchen table and will instantly spruce up an afternoon klatch with a friend or two. It's equally lovely on a low coffee table, bringing a small touch of elegance to the living room, where you might serve cocktails or coffee and dessert to your guests. Even a bedroom can benefit from this graceful type of bouquet—guests will be delighted to find this simple, bright addition to the spare bedroom when they arrive for the weekend.

With their short yet cylindrical shape, these cups easily double as vases and have a clean, modern look. Use caution when clipping the roses for this type of arrangement. If you cut the stems too short the flowers will be top heavy and fall over; the rose heads need some stem to hold each other up.

Most kitchen stores these days carry a simple Asian tea set such as this one; the crimson roses create a beautiful color contrast with the cream-colored glaze. I also recommend experimenting with tea sets in various colors and textures, for there are endless pretty combinations. Try pairing beautiful apricot garden roses such as 'Evelyn' with a bronze Asian tea set, or lavender roses such as 'Paradise' with a set in the classic Blue Willow pattern.

You can also seek out a more old-fashioned, multicolored tea set for a look that's evocative of afternoon tea in an English garden. Keep in mind, however, that it can be challenging to get flowers to stay put in the more traditional teacups, which are quite shallow. In this case, the best approach is to fill the cup with water almost to the rim, and simply float the flower head on the surface. If you're using only one flower per teacup you may want to create an echo effect by using a series of cups: place them on a tray laid with a pretty napkin, setting the cups in a circle around the teapot, or in a vertical line adjacent to it.

41

- *'Traviata' roses*
- *'Enigma' roses*
- *'Black Magic' roses*

## Simple Rose Bowls

The layered, whorled, circular petal arrangement in these especially beautiful red roses is a work of art in itself. Placing the blossoms in bowls—in this case, 1950s vintage bowls the color of new grass—puts the spotlight on their extraordinarily rich color and complex shape.

This simple, elegant display of rose blossoms has a distinctly chic, modern flair, but in fact it's a decorative approach that has been appreciated by rosarians for nearly a century. In 1910, the author of *British Floral Decoration*, Robert Felton, a leading florist in London at that time, recommended a natural style of arranging, proclaiming his distaste for the "prim dwarfed bunches of flowers" in fashion during the mid-nineteenth century. The wonderful book *Flora Domestica* (see Bibliography) reprints his advice, which still rings true: ". . . if you wish to get the best effect from a great bunch of roses, arrange them in a rose-bowl on a low table where you can look down into their very hearts." Credited with bringing down the scale of arrangements, Mr. Felton started a trend that today is still very much in vogue. This display of rose blooms, entirely detached from the stems, takes this advice and concept to the fullest extent. Because the spotlight is entirely on the blossoms, you'll want to seek out roses that are fully open and possessed of a luxuriant petal formation. The types used here can be relied on for beautiful results, and two of them—the 'Enigma' rose and the 'Black Magic' rose—are hothouse varieties that can be ordered from a florist throughout the year. These two varieties are among my favorite hothouse roses; they resemble garden roses in their lush, circular petal arrangement (if you put your finger in the rose's center, you can trace the path of the rows to come out at the flower's rim). But I couldn't resist adding a true garden rose, the 'Traviata', to the bowls. If you can't find it, however, the bowls will still look lovely with just the two hothouse varieties. The 'Traviata' is a very full rose that performs brilliantly in the spotlight and needs no adornment to delight the eye.

While a single bowl of these crimson roses would be simply lovely, a series of them increases the impact and creates a more memorable look.

42

You can line the center of a long dinner table with the blossom-filled bowls for a special occasion, or scatter them about a room that you're decorating for a cocktail party. You can add some bowls with floating candles or simply light a few votives on the table for an intimate look. These vintage Paul McCobb bowls from the 1950s have a striking form that's especially appropriate for holding several rose blossoms at once. Nothing is required to make them stay in place. When you are clipping off the heads of the roses, clip them at the nape, just a little below where the stem attaches to the bulbous base of the rose head.

I usually choose a monochromatic palette, as in this case where roses have subtly varying shades of crimson, but experimenting with a mix of colors can also yield beautiful results. With monochromatic arrangements, it's very effective to use containers or table linens in complementary colors. For example, bowls of lavender roses would look gorgeous with sky-blue linens, while fiery orange blossoms would glow against a tablecloth of vivid yellow. Bowls of flowers are a cinch to keep up; replenish the water level when it starts to dip and you should be able to enjoy the gorgeous floating blooms for up to 5 days.

43

Pink

# Pink

47

- *'Secret' roses*
- *'Auguste Renoir' roses*
- *'Yves Piaget' roses*
- *Wired pink ribbon*

## BRIDAL PINK

The radiant glow of pink flowers in a bride's hands as she walks down the aisle is traditional and invariably gorgeous. It's no wonder a ribbon-tied posy of these romantic garden roses has become the classic bridal bouquet. Whether your choice is a soft, delicate pastel or a rich, vibrant pink, this fresh and beautiful color is a natural match for the momentous occasion.

This bouquet of roses creates the picture of bridal charm using roses in a medley of pink. The full, shapely 'Secret' rose is a blend of several hues, with shading from a creamy pinkish-white center to petals edged in delicate, radiant pink. The many-petaled 'Auguste Renoir' rose, a Romantica Hybrid Tea, is a strong, deep pink that vibrates with an almost bluish intensity. The 'Yves Piaget', a Romantica Hybrid Tea, has a rich fragrance and beautiful pink hue with a tinge of mauve. The color is subtler than that of the bright 'Auguste Renoir', but the shape is dramatic, with deeply cupped blooms that resemble those of a peony. Bridal bouquets are really best made with garden roses, since they capture a lushness that is appropriate for the occasion and have an evocative fragrance. But should garden roses be in short supply, hothouse varieties can be substituted: for the creamy pink, seek out 'Anna',

'Dolce Vita', or 'Nicole' roses; for deep, solid pink, look for 'Hot Princess' or 'Titanic' roses. When it comes to wrapping the bouquet in ribbon, I prefer a rich, beautiful color like the deep, glowing fuchsia shown here—it creates a striking contrast with a traditional white wedding dress.

The best way to assemble a bridal bouquet is to start with the preparation. First, cut the heads off the stems—it may seem unnatural to do this but it's necessary if you'll be attaching wire. Detach the rose head at the stem just below the bulbous part of the flower. (Wire will run through the bulbous part, so be sure it does not get attached.) The next step is to wire the head of each rose with an 18-inch length of 20- or 22-gauge piece of wire: Insert the wire into the base of the rose horizontally until the rose is in the middle of the wire. Then bend down both ends of the wire to form a single false wire stem. Next, wrap

48

the wire in floral tape from the top down, pulling the tape taut as you go, covering the wire completely. (Floral tape sticks to itself but not to your fingers; you can buy it in floral shops.) This makes the wire sturdier and camouflages it as well. When all the wire stems are taped, begin constructing the bouquet by bunching your color choices together. (I tend to cluster like colors together, in this case by putting the cream-colored 'Secret' roses together at the center and surrounding them with the brighter-colored 'Yves Piaget' and 'Auguste Renoir'.) Tape each bunch together down the wire stems, once again pulling the tape taut as you go. Once these bunches are complete, join them together and tape them into one bouquet. If you plan to use floral preservatives for additional lasting power, mist the bouquet at this point—I use Crowning Glory, which can be purchased at wholesale flower supply stores (or through a local florist). Make sure that the Crowning Glory is completely dry before you tie up the bouquet. The last step is easy: while someone else gently holds the finished bouquet, wrap it in wired ribbon from the top down.

49

- *Orange dahlias*
- *Pink zinnias*
- *'Latin Ambience' roses*
- *'Secret' roses*

## BIRTHDAY PARTY

Whether you're a kid, or just a kid at heart, a birthday is best celebrated with close friends, delicious treats, and a few surprises. The vibrant flowers and bright patterns of this display capture the mischievous and light-hearted spirit of the occasion. Setting the stage is as simple as creating an easy flower arrangement, presenting a few gifts wrapped with tissue paper and bright-colored ribbon, and singing "Happy Birthday" before it's time to blow out the candles.

When it comes to experimenting with color, look to round-headed zinnias and dramatic, fluffy dahlias, which offer a dazzling array of choices and are always terrific paired with roses. Here, the hot-pink zinnias may seem like an unexpected match for the bright-orange dahlias, but the combination creates a fun, playful mood. The 'Latin Ambience' rose has beautiful, full-cupped blossoms with an interesting petal formation; although it resembles a garden rose, it's actually a hothouse variety you can order from a florist year-round. This particular arrangement is most easily made in late summer and fall, when roses, zinnias, and dahlias are generally available. Depending upon what's in season, however, you can shift the balance of zinnias or dahlias using more of one or the other, and vary the color within that single variety. If you have trouble finding orange, try using yellow and pink for another unexpected color pairing that adds to a festive mood. Or, in spring, when orange dahlias may be scarce, you can substitute long-lasting scarlet peonies for the orange dahlias.

Achieving this cheerful look involves drawing a tabletop together with bright colors in the flowers, linens, dishes, and gift wrap. There's always plenty to do to get ready for a party, and one of the virtues of this arrangement is that it can be thrown together quickly. Holding the stems in one hand, I begin with the dahlias, then add the roses, and next the zinnias, finally cutting the stems to approximately the same length, always on the diagonal so the stems can easily

draw up water. Using tissue paper and bright-colored ribbon that either picks up the hues of the flowers or provides festive contrast (as the pale blue packages in the background do here), I wrap the gifts. With the addition of polka-dotted table linens and a few simple dishes with a pretty glaze, everything is ready to go. Don't be afraid to experiment with bright colors. It only takes a little effort, and the extra zing is worth it.

51

- *'Gertrude Jekyll' roses*
- *Lilies of the valley*

## CONGRATULATIONS IN PINK

I'm always spellbound by the classic pink color, intoxicating scent, and perfect rose shape of 'Gertrude Jekyll'. When they're combined with aromatic lilies of the valley, the result is a riot of freshness that evokes a fabulous garden—and captures a spirit of new beginnings. The arrangement is perfect for a congratulatory celebration, whether the happy occasion is an engagement party or an elegant baby shower.

Some flowers stand head and shoulders above the rest due to their elegance and femininity. Such is the case with the 'Gertrude Jekyll', which carries one of the strongest perfumes of all the English roses and boasts full, rosette-shaped blossoms that embody "old rose" characteristics. Named after a famous English gardener, this beautiful David Austin flower is the heart and soul of this arrangement. However, if you don't have access to the variety, you can substitute pink peonies in spring or pink tulips in winter. Lily of the valley, with its long history as a bridal favorite, is an appealing partner for the roses. The waxy, delicate, bell-shaped white flowers emit a sweet perfume and, along with their broad, green leaves, provide textural and color contrast with the roses. Due to the numerous roses and the cost of lilies of the valley, this arrangement's price adds up quickly. If you want to keep the cost down, substitute some less expensive flowers, such as pink carnations, for either of the other two varieties—it will still look gorgeous. (Another benefit of using carnations is that, unlike lilies of the valley, they create a voluminous base for the rest of the arrangement.) But when it comes to making the small satellite arrangements—here, one is composed of lilies of the valley while two are mostly roses—use the finest blooms in the bunch. Satellite displays enhance the effect of the main arrangement, but they also draw the eye and give each bloom a chance to shine on its own.

I'm always accumulating new clear glass containers, since they are easy to find in all shapes and sizes. Having this wide variety of vessels is extremely helpful when an occasion

53

calls for a large display with smaller satellite arrangements, as shown here. It's a simple presentation that makes any occasion elegant. If you prefer, skip the large arrangement and go for the more subtle effect of displaying numerous small bouquets in petite glass vases. Gift boxes, wrapped in festive striped paper and tied with bright pink bows, and festive glassware add to the anticipation of party fun.

If you do choose to create the large display, make sure you begin arranging with the vase in its final resting spot, in order to avoid the hassle and potential disruption of your design from carrying the heavy load from one place to another. I make this large arrangement by simply putting the flowers in the vase, first placing the roses, and then sliding in the lilies of the valley. After years of arranging, I place flowers by instinct, but novice arrangers can start by placing the lilies of the valley in triangles surrounding each rose, or by simply filling in with blooms wherever you spot an obvious hole. The satellite arrangements are wonderfully easy to make. Mimic the technique described for a larger arrangement.

- *'Bewitched' roses*
- *'Auguste Renoir' roses*
- *'Secret' roses*
- *'Tiffany' roses*
- *'Yves Piaget' roses*

## PINK CLASSIC

After assembling this display of lush pink roses outside on a summer afternoon, I just couldn't bear to bring it indoors. Set on a beautiful, old garden chair, the arrangement reminds me of a rustic farmhouse garden in Provence. There's real charm to flowers in an outdoor setting, where the natural light and earthy surroundings make the colors glow and pop.

This assemblage of showy, vibrant blossoms represents something of an A-list of pink roses. Composed of three modern Hybrid Teas and two Romantica roses, this bouquet shows the stunning beauty that can be achieved with a monochromatic color scheme. Each of the five varieties has a slightly different shape, color intensity, and fragrance. (If you have trouble finding any of the specific roses named here, seek out a rose with similar qualities.) The 'Bewitched' rose, sometimes described as a "show rose" for its beautifully formed, ruffly petals, has a good fragrance and pale pink color. A Hybrid Tea rose called 'Secret', a recent arrival in the world of pink roses that dates to 1992, is a vision of a shimmering pale pink. The petals are often edged with slightly darker pink, and they carry a sweet-spicy fragrance. When it comes to scent, however, few roses can compare with the 'Tiffany' rose, which won the prestigious James Alexander Gamble Fragrance Medal from the American Rose Society (the award is bestowed upon top-performing intensely fragrant roses). This Hybrid Tea rose dates to 1954 and has large, elegant classic Hybrid Tea–shaped buds that open to moderately full, cotton-candy-pink blossoms. The two Romantica roses in this arrangement, 'Auguste Renoir' and 'Yves Piaget', are remarkable not only for color but for their frilly, many-petaled, peonylike blossoms. Each is a "full" rose, meaning that its blossom has between 26 and 40 petals. (In contrast, most Hybrid Tea roses, such as those mentioned above, tend to carry "double" blossoms, which have between 17 and 25 petals.) This endows them with a notable lush and luxuriant appearance. Both of these Romantica roses are a true, deep pink. The large flowers of the 'Yves Piaget'

55

can grow to up to 6 inches across. These are all garden roses, which may not be available all through the year. If you're looking for hothouse pink roses, which are available year-round, consider the 'Nicole' rose.

This classic, urn-shaped glass vase does a wonderful job of raising the flowers up without detracting from them, so nothing interferes with the outstanding pink blossoms that star in this display. I found this container in a small boutique. If you don't have a similar vase on hand, just head out to the nearby pet store and buy the biggest fish bowl they have. Creating this display is a challenge because of the sheer number of roses, so novice arrangers might start with a smaller version. When you're working with this many roses, the most time-consuming step is going to be "processing" the roses—in other words, stripping them of leaves and thorns. Using a rose stripper and protective gloves, remove the thorns from each stem,

working patiently on one stem at a time. Removing thorns is especially important when you're putting a large volume of stems into a small container such as this classic urn-shaped vase, because thorns can make it difficult to place the rose stems closely together. I made this arrangement right in the vase, and I suggest that you do the same. If you're having trouble keeping the stems from falling out try using chicken wire (see page 20) to secure them. It's best to begin with 4 flowers (at north, south, east, and west positions) at the far outer edges of the bowl and work inward, building the roses up in each corner and then filling in the empty spaces until you have a complete arrangement. The wonderful aspect of monochromatic arrangements such as this one is that putting the flowers together is virtually foolproof; the pink color base allows the roses to look natural together no matter how you place them.

- *'Color of Magic' roses*
- *'Perdita' roses*
- *Peach dahlias*
- *Scarlet dahlias*

## DAHLIA'S PINK

Just because flowers come with stems attached doesn't mean they have to stay that way. Some of my favorite arrangements highlight fully opened blooms that have been clipped at the nape. Lush dahlias take on an exotic appearance, almost like a sea creature, when pressed against the glass of this flower-packed vase. Whether you use de-stemmed flowers in an unexpected, creative way as shown here, or simply float a rose in a glazed ceramic bowl, it's an approach that lavishes attention on the beautiful solitary blossoms.

At my local flower market in mid-October, the dahlias are at their biggest and most mature. I'm always brainstorming creative new ways to take advantage of their beauty in this glorious, transient state. One such experiment, in which I beheaded and submerged the dahlias in water to disguise a handful of rose stems, turned the bouquet into a modern and whimsical piece. It's best to seek out full, almost showy, roses for the arrangement, or they might look rather small and unremarkable next to the oversized dahlias. The 'Perdita' rose, a David Austin English variety named after one of the heroines of Shakespeare's play *The Winter's Tale*, has perfect rosette-shaped flowers and a strong English-rose and myrrh (slightly spicy) fragrance. Its pale, glowing color is best described as apricot

blush. The name of the 'Color of Magic' rose is indicative of the flower's beauty. This modern Hybrid Tea has beautiful creamy petals in variegated deep and pale pink. The arrangement of these flowers is one that's suitable for entertaining, whether it adorns a dining room sideboard, mantel, or living room table.

Using a classic glass vase in a cylindrical shape is the key to this arrangement—the diameter should be approximately 6 to 8 inches wide to accommodate the flower stems as well as the voluminous beheaded dahlias. (Note that a V-shaped container with a a narrow base and wide mouth simply won't work.) This arrangement will end up being quite heavy, so seek out a vase of thin glass rather than the weighty, thick-walled variety. (I always carry vases with

both hands, holding them at the bottom—never carry a vase by the neck or the lip. I've learned this the hard way, not just by breaking the vase but by cutting my hand!) Before making the arrangement, set aside 8 dahlias for the arrangement and 4 dahlias to behead. When you clip the rose stems, leave them a bit longer than the dahlia stems since they will be at the center and the highest point of the arrangement. The first step is to fill the vase halfway with water and sink the beheaded dahlias below the surface. Be sure they create enough coverage to disguise all the rose stems. I was surprised to discover that they need something to weigh them down or they float right up to the top; my solution was to use clear glass Christmas balls. If you don't have these on hand, try using marbles in the largest size—these are available from many Web sites, and most craft stores offer some variety. Finally, put the dahlias with stems still attached along the outer edge and fill in the center with roses; group at least 2 or 3 blooms of each rose type together for maximum impact. If you can't find scarlet and peach dahlias, you can substitute red and pink, which are usually easy to find. Seasonal alternatives to the dahlias include peonies in spring and hydrangeas in summer. If you're going to behead the blossoms, however, peonies are the only truly good substitute because they hold their shape off the stem.

59

- *'Leonidas' roses*
- *'Gypsi Curiosa' roses*
- *'Sahara' roses*
- *'Evelyn' roses*

## ANTIQUE SILVER AND PINK

Silver and pink create a beautiful, formal mood that is perfectly suited to sophisticated entertaining. I prefer the antique look of tarnished silver, since I like to avoid using shiny pieces that compete with the flowers for attention. These elegant old ice buckets, with their imperfect but still reflective exteriors, provide fitting containers for these roses, which include David Austin's 'Evelyn'. This magnificent bloom has "old rose" characteristics and carries one of the most intoxicating fragrances of all the English roses.

Now that it's possible to get roses in earthy colors, such as the cinnamon 'Leonidas' rose, or the beige 'Sahara' rose, I find myself increasingly reliant on them to bring warmth and depth to arrangements. These two particular roses, as well as the 'Gypsi Curiosa', which is pink with tints of soft, rosy brown, are grown in hothouses year-round and should be readily available from your local florist. The colors appear exceedingly natural yet are recent arrivals; the 'Leonidas', one of my favorites among the warm earthy-toned roses, is a Hybrid Tea that was just introduced in 1995. For this display, I've paired a selection of earthy-toned blooms with apricot pink 'Evelyn', a David Austin rose. Any arrangement that stars this large, old-fashioned beauty is bound to elicit gasps of delight, and the rose's tendency toward color and shape variation means it never has a cookie-cutter appearance. For example, the color of 'Evelyn' is sometimes a blend of apricot and yellow infused with a hint of pink, while at other times the bloom looks pure pink. Its shape can vary, from a broad, shallow cup with petals turning upward around the edges to a perfect, full rosette. The 'Evelyn' resonates beautifully against the soft, warm brown undertones of the other roses here, but if it's not available, you can pair the earthy blossoms with a big, dramatic red bloom that is fully open. If you have access to garden roses, try David Austin's beautiful crimson 'L. D. Braithwaite'; among hothouse varieties, the 'Black Beauty' rose might be a nice choice.

61

Check in those dusty hideaways like an attic and find any ice buckets you may have stowed away. They make wonderful containers for flowers, whether they come in the elegant shape of an urn with handles or a more traditional bucket shape. If you don't have any on hand, keep your eyes peeled for silver pieces when you visit antique stores. An urn made of terra-cotta, the type often found in garden centers, could act as a substitute in a pinch. The urn-shaped container used here elevates the flowers as if on a pedestal, making a stunning bouquet for a festive buffet, or as a centerpiece at a dinner party.

With these types of containers, I use Oasis floral foam to hold the stems in place. The first step is to submerge the Oasis in water until it is very heavy (about 10 minutes) and then mash it up with your fingers to create a pile of pebble-sized bits. Place the foam at the bottom of the ice bucket, fill the container with water, and then add the flowers. The dome silhouette of the flowers naturally complements the uplifted, triangular shape of the urn. To create this rounded arrangement, cut some of the rose stems longer than the others. Make the arrangement in the container—it's so easy to do when you're using Oasis. Group colors together for the maximum color impact. A dining room table adorned with toile, as shown here, and set with old-fashioned china and crystal provides the perfect background for the antique charm of this arrangement.

- *Pink hydrangeas*
- *Green hydrangeas*
- *'Jade' roses*
- *'Gertrude Jekyll' roses*

## PINK AND GREEN ENTRYWAY

A fabulous green Italian vase from the 1950s inspired this eye-catching arrangement. I've loved the preppy green-and-pink combination since I was a kid and couldn't resist the chance to recreate that palette with roses and hydrangeas in this unusual vessel. While this color combination isn't exactly common among floral displays, it always looks fresh. On a color wheel, green is the complement of red, and pink is simply a tint of red; as a result, pink and green are natural partners that look sweet together.

Entryways can be transformed quickly with the addition of flowers. To really make the space come to life, I seek out tall containers and fill them with vivid, showy blooms. This often-neglected part of the house is an ideal place to showcase unusual containers (such as this vintage piece) that would overwhelm a more intimate space, such as a dining room or kitchen. If you have a container that just never looks quite right elsewhere in the house, it might look just right here. (Just keep in mind that because entryway spaces often lack a natural focal point, small, low arrangements can easily go unnoticed.) Fluffy, colorful hydrangeas are a good choice to pair with roses when you're creating a display that needs volume. Here, the green hydrangea enhances the impact of the soft emerald 'Jade' roses, while the pink hydrangea echoes the hues of the vibrant 'Gertrude Jekyll'. If you have trouble finding this particular garden rose, a David Austin English rose, you can substitute another vibrant pink blossom such as 'Dolce Vita' or 'Titanic'. Since hydrangeas also come in other hues, including white, lavender, and blue, you could easily alter the color palette of this arrangement. Instead of showcasing pink and green, for example, you could use a white and lavender color scheme using white and lavender hydrangea, 'Akito' (white) roses, and 'Sterling' (lavender) roses, which are generally easy to find. If you wish to make the arrangement in the spring, lilacs are a wonderful substitute.

63

Finding containers with unique dimensions takes a little bit of work, but the result is well worth the effort. Antique shops and flea markets are good places to find vintage pieces. I'm particularly drawn to opaque colored-glass containers. Whether their color is red, pink, orange, or green, they constantly inspire ideas for flower displays, (you can match the flowers to the color of the glass, or create a vivid color contrast with blooms in a complementary color). A tall, elongated container such as this one has just the right dimensions for a hall or entryway; urns are also a good choice because they raise the flowers up on a pedestal and make them more noticeable. Another way to increase the drama is to put the vase before a mirror or in front of a lamp that is tall and in proportion to the flowers. If you're looking for a good alternative to colored glass, try a tall silver vase or a ceramic container in a fluted square or rectangle. For a clean and modern look, a tall frosted-glass cylinder is nice.

This arrangement couldn't be easier to create. The fat, clustered hydrangea blossoms create a good base for the roses, allowing you to make the arrangement without the aid of floral foam or wire. The first step is to place the hydrangeas in the vase, then place the roses in, putting the tallest flowers in the center to achieve the dome shape shown here. A nice final touch is to place a small dish filled with rose petals next to it, softening the look of the arrangement and bringing even more color to the space.

White

# White

69

- *'Swan' roses*
- *'Vendela' roses*
- *Calla lilies*
- *Cream-colored velvet ribbon*

## TRADITIONAL BRIDE

Wedding gowns provide stunning examples of the many shades of white, from nearly reflective satin and cream-colored heirloom lace to frothy white tulle. The roses in this traditional bridal bouquet have the delicacy of fine fabric, and the mixture of cream and white echoes the subtle variation of colors you might see in a classic bridal ensemble.

With its deep-cupped blossom and pure white color, the 'Swan' garden rose makes a wonderfully romantic centerpiece for this bouquet. If you have trouble finding this variety but have access to other garden roses, you could substitute 'Fair Bianca', a David Austin garden rose with a pretty cupped shape and lovely white petals that have just a hint of cream. The other rose in this bouquet, the cream-colored 'Vendela', has a more classic narrow, Hybrid Tea shape. It's cultivated in hothouses and can generally be ordered year-round. The white blossoms are the perfect foil for the warm, peachy color of the calla lilies, which enliven the bouquet with their satiny texture and elegant, fluted shape. The color here is so vibrant it almost looks dyed, but callas grow naturally in such shades as a result of hybridization, in colors ranging from hot pink, orange, and crimson to burgundy and black. Fresh callas can easily last for hours out of water. This makes them a favorite for bridal bouquets, which need to maintain their freshness and beauty throughout the celebratory day. They're also a great choice for a boutonniere.

Making this bridal bouquet requires a bit of patience and dexterity, not to mention a few hours, but the astonishingly beautiful results are well worth the effort. The first step is to behead the roses, detaching the head of each blossom at the baldest part of the stem just below the base of the flower. The next step is to wire the head of each rose: insert an 18-inch long, 22-gauge piece of wire horizontally into the base of the rose until the base is at the middle of the wire. Then bend down both sides of the wire to form a single wire stem. Next, wrap the wire in floral tape from the top down, stretching the tape as you go down and covering the wire

70

completely. (Floral tape sticks to itself but not to your fingers; you can buy it in floral shops.) You will not need to wire the calla lilies, which have extremely sturdy stems. Once each of the wire-stemmed roses is taped, begin constructing the bouquet by bunching your color choices together. Tape each bunch, wrapping the tape around the wire stems, once again pulling the tape as you go down. When these bunches are complete, join them together and tape them into one bouquet. If you plan to use floral preservatives for additional lasting power, mist the bouquet at this point—I use Crowning Glory, which can be purchased at wholesale flower supply stores (or through a local florist). Make sure none of the spray gets onto the ribbon you'll be using, and that the Crowning Glory is completely dry before you tie up the bouquet. Once the flowers are ready to go, have someone else hold the bouquet as you add a cream-colored velvet ribbon in a criss-cross formation, wrapping from the top and progressing down. I prefer to leave the ribbon tails long rather than tying them in a bow, so they can flutter in the bride's hands as she walks down the aisle.

*A Bouquet of Roses*

*'Akito' roses*

*'Avalanche' roses*

*Blue hydrangeas*

*White scabiosa*

*Succulent plants*

## BEACHY FRESH

The soft blue and white seascape around Eastern Long Island, where I spend part of the summer, inspired this lush arrangement. The freshness of the colors captures the feeling of the season, and the generous size and shape of the full-headed white 'Avalanche' roses remind me of the abundant blooms so often seen in rose gardens in July and August. Keeping this beautiful arrangement around the house during the warm months reminds me of bare feet, bike rides, and sundresses—all the joys of summer.

'Akito' roses are an excellent choice when you're seeking white blossoms because of the purity of their color and their lovely, elegant shape. The 'Avalanche' roses, also white, have fuller blossoms and give the bouquet an unmistakable lushness. Both of these hothouse roses should be readily available; if you have trouble finding them, you can request them from your local floral shop. White scabiosa, the wonderful summer flowers that round out the arrangement, are generally easy to find in the warm months. The delicate petals capture light, while the pincushion centers add a bit of texture. The densely packed style of this arrangement really highlights the gorgeous blossoms. This bouquet is quick and easy to create—the best type of bouquet for a warm day when you'd rather wriggle your toes in the sand than fuss over flowers. With its classic blue and white combination, and seashells scattered about the base, this bouquet practically conjures up the salty ocean air. The arrangement would be a gorgeous addition to a bright, airy beach house, but it truly needs no other occasion than a clear summer day.

When I'm creating a densely packed arrangement, I start with a base of voluminous flowers that helps anchor the roses. I almost always use hydrangeas as a base because they come in an array of gorgeous colors, and there's usually one that is well matched to my arrangement. In this case, this shade of soft blue seemed just perfect. Don't be afraid to clip off most of the stems; you don't need much length if you're using a bowl as a container. And you

73

don't need to worry about using floral foam or tape to keep things in place. Filled with water, most bowls have the width to contain several flowers without the help of any props.

The first step in making the bouquet is to place the hydrangeas at the outer circumference of the arrangement: their voluminous blossoms help to camouflage the rim of the bowl. The depth of the container you use will dictate how much to clip from the stems of the roses and scabiosa; better to leave them too long than too short, since you can't add length back, and too-short stems will be unable to reach the water. With the hydrangea at the outer circumference of the container, fill in the central space with roses, and then add the white scabiosa. With all the flowers in place, add a few green succulents to provide color contrast and an interesting texture. Note how the flowers spill over and hide the rim of the thick-walled glass bowl to create a soft, natural look. Because the container reminded me of beach glass, and the pale blue color echoed the azure hue of the hydrangeas, it seemed like the perfect vessel for these flowers. However, nearly any bowl can work in this type of arrangement, even the Pyrex glass version—just pile in the flowers, place it on a table, and it will look gorgeous. (Nobody will guess it's the same bowl you mixed the cake batter in!) I like the Turkish towel beneath the bowl because it creates a sort of frame for the arrangement. You can use any fabric, even something with fringe, as long as the color or pattern isn't so bright that it attracts attention away from the flowers.

## FLOATING LIGHT

Sometimes the simplest use of flowers brings the greatest pleasure. This is the case with rose blooms afloat in water. Often, flowers are paired with floating candles in table decorations, but I think the effect is most stunning when they appear in unexpected places such as this lovely stone birdbath. Any visitor wandering through the garden who discovered this luminous sight would find it completely enchanting.

Rosy beige 'Sahara' roses, accompanied by 'White Majolika' spray roses, create a picture of loveliness when set adrift in this pool of water. The difference in shape between the two varieties—spray roses are miniatures while the Sahara roses have full-sized blossoms—adds visual interest, as do the floating candles. The display is lovely in white, but you could easily choose another color scheme, such as lavender: try seeking out a vibrant variety, such as the full-cupped 'Paul Neyron' rose, a garden variety that is available throughout the summer. You can contrast this with any variety of lavender hothouse rose. Floating candles come in a wide range of colors can be found everywhere from craft shops to upscale home stores. No matter what shade of flowers and candles you choose, rest assured that their subtle beauty will be the hit of any outdoor party or garden walk.

The correct place to detach the rose heads in order to keep them fresh and pretty is just below the bulbous section under the bloom, nearly at the top of the stem. Once the rose blooms are off the stems, creating this display is as simple as it looks. Just float the flowers and candles in the water, lighting the wicks right before your guests arrive. If you don't have a stone birdbath or other similar garden adornment to use as a vessel, don't despair. Garden centers generally stock a wide array of rustic containers in terracotta, stone, and even fiberglass (try to find one that's been painted white, or paint it yourself with spray paint). Shapes range from wide, shallow basins to planter boxes, and virtually any type will work for this purpose. If there are holes in the bottom, use a plastic liner to keep the water from draining. One benefit to using easily movable containers is that you can create

a series of 4 or 5 Floating Light arrangements and place them around the patio, deck, yard, or anywhere outside that is deserving. On a summer evening, your guests will most likely arrive when it's still light out; as dusk settles in, you can light the candles and bring illumination and intimacy to your alfresco party.

77

*Clematis vines*
*'Avalanche' roses*
*'Akito' roses*

## D ε c a d ε n t   C a n d ε l a b r a

The key piece in this arrangement is the silver candelabra, a cherished heirloom in my family. Adorned with some winding clematis vines and a few well-placed roses, it creates a striking and elegant centerpiece. Not only does it provide a unique base for an arrangement, but it also allows you to put your candles and your flowers all in one place. If you don't have a candelabra, keep your eyes open when you visit flea markets and antique shops. They're not all that difficult to find and, with a little effort, you may discover the perfect heirloom yourself.

Antique silver, with its slightly tarnished patina, always conveys old-world elegance. When presented alongside white blossoms, the overall effect is one of reflection and illumination. The white 'Akito' and 'Avalanche' roses used here are available year-round, which gives this arrangement a wonderful versatility. It's the perfect choice for an alfresco dinner party in the summer, when you could easily substitute honeysuckle or passionflower for the clematis vines. The arrangement can work equally well in other seasons, too, and can even be a gorgeous addition to your winter holiday table; in the cold months you can replace the clematis with ivy or small branches of greenery such as white pine or olive leaf. Mixing a few deep-red roses, such as 'Enigma' roses or 'Black Magic' roses (both of these beautiful hothouse roses are available in the winter), in with the white blossoms creates a festive mood. No matter when you display this creation, the dramatic backdrop of the candelabra will always elicit "ooohs" and "ahhhs" from your friends.

While the arrangement looks sophisticated and elegant, it's surprisingly easy to create. You can have fun making it, just tossing the clematis (or whatever vine you're using) around the candelabra and winding it through the spaces. Using your instinct to determine their ideal location, place the roses into the little crevices

78

created by the looping vine, wrapping them in place with small cuts of pipe cleaners (chenilles). The chenilles, whose soft surface won't scratch the candelabra, are necessary because without them, the roses would look droopy and ruin the effect. Chenilles are easily sourced at a craft supply store. Once you master this arrangement, it may quickly become a favorite. It's easy, it creates a memorable statement, and it offers the opportunity to put aside your usual dinner party vase and showcase the candelabra. A loose, relaxed look is part of the arrangement's charm, so don't worry about getting the vine or the flowers perfectly placed. This arrangement should look more wild and unruly than tidy, as if it is a vine in an abandoned secret garden.

*'Honor' roses*
*White hydrangeas*
*Peach amaryllis*
*Lady's mantle*
*Tuberose*

## WHITE ENTRYWAY

White is a cool, inviting color that is perfect for adorning an entryway, particularly when it's enhanced with subtle texture contrasts and a single shot of bright, peachy color. The smooth satin finish of garden roses, the feathery lace-cap look of hydrangeas, the rounded leaves of lady's mantle, and the wonderfully fragrant tuberose provide a beautiful white background for the showy peach amaryllis.

This tall, glamorous flower display takes center stage in an entryway and welcomes guests into the house with its rosy peach and white color scheme. When making a tall, lavish arrangement such as this one, the key is to use a wide-mouthed glass vase with plenty of height so you can pack in lots of flowers. The 'Honor' rose, a beautiful Hybrid Tea, is a wonderful choice for this showcase because of its pure, snow-white color and shapely blossoms. The rose was chosen as an All-American Rose Selection in 1980. (Bill Warriner, the hybridizer of 'Honor', swept the All-American Rose Selections that year by winning with two other roses: 'Love' in the Grandiflora category and 'Cherish' in the Floribunda category.) If you have trouble finding 'Honor' roses (they can be impossible to come by once the summer has passed), substitute white hothouse varieties such as 'Akito'. These don't carry the same classic fragrance as the 'Honor' roses, but they offer a similarly pure white color. As long as you include the elegant, creamy tuberose, which carries a heady, delicious scent, the room will be filled with a wonderful perfume. The hydrangeas add volume to the arrangement, draping over the vase rim to camouflage the stems of other flowers. In spring, you can replace the white hydrangeas with fluffy white peonies or lilacs. I like the shape contrast provided by amaryllis, which is widely available in shops in the winter months. You could also use any other pink or peach lily. Lady's mantle, with its clusters of rounded, pale yellow-green leaves, adds a rustic-garden touch to the otherwise refined look of this display. If

81

you can't cut lady's mantle from your own garden in the spring and summer months, you might try substituting a flowering herb such as thyme or even try ivy. As always, if you can't find the exact shades recommended, go ahead and experiment. It's certainly possible to switch the color of each individual flower and still achieve the same overall look; for example, you could substitute white amaryllis or white 'Casablanca' lilies for the peach amaryllis, or you could replace the white 'Honor' roses with a pink garden variety such as 'Tiffany'.

By the time you complete it, this arrangement will be large and quite heavy. For this reason, you should always make large arrangements on site; in other words, place the vase in its final location and bring the flowers there to arrange them. (Begin with an empty vase; fill it with water before the flowers are placed in order to avoid a spill while you're working.) If you make the arrangement elsewhere and then move it, the flowers you've worked so hard to balance can get out of whack as you carry them. Even

though this arrangement is tall and imposing, you don't need Oasis or floral wire to keep it in place, because the hydrangeas act as a base flower. When you're cutting the stems, think about the architecture of the display: the roses and amaryllis should have longer stems than the hydrangeas.

This arrangement might look daunting but it's actually easier to make than a small, densely packed display. The flowers can easily be assembled in the container. Begin by putting some hydrangeas at the outer edges of the container. Add the 'Honor' roses, fill in with more hydrangeas, build up height with the amaryllis and tuberose, and then top it off with a scattering of lady's mantle. The longer-stemmed flowers will be in the middle, while the shorter-stemmed hydrangeas will cover up the lip of the vase and hide the remainder of the stems coming out of the vase, which could detract from the blossoms.

# Yellow & Green

# Yellow & Green

- *'Gina Lollobrigida' roses*
- *Miniature field daisies*
- *Queen Anne's lace*
- *Wheat-colored grass stalks*

## WILDFLOWER CELEBRATION

Golden sunlight falling across a summer field dotted with white Queen Anne's lace, tiny daisies, and pretty, delicate asters inspired this bouquet. Part of the beauty of the arrangement is its utter simplicity. These wild-flowers, which are naturally bright and luminous, look especially stunning with yellow roses. They could also look lovely with 'Jade' roses, which are a soft emerald color, or orange roses such as 'Rio Samba'.

The 'Gina Lollobrigida' rose, a French hybrid, has a rich, golden color and wonderful rose fragrance. In this bouquet, its abundant cupped blooms create volume to compensate for the tall, leggy Queen Anne's lace. If you have trouble finding the 'Gina Lollobrigida', a garden rose, the 'Skyline' hothouse variety can be a good substitute. A few wheat-colored grass stalks can be gathered up with the wildflowers to add height and rustic charm to the arrangement. All the wildflowers shown here will need to be picked fresh from a field, since floral shops rarely carry them. However, good substitutes such as daisies or sunflowers can be found at flower markets. Other options include black-eyed Susans (usually easy to find at shops in summer), larkspurs, belladonna delphiniums, or any of the different types and colors of asters.

Whatever flowers you use, this simple and casual arrangement is just as gorgeous in the kitchen, where its sunny colors and appealing shape can be enjoyed from morning until night.

Pairing this rustic urn with wildflowers is a good example of how to create a mood with your container. I found it one day while browsing in an antique store in rural Massachusetts and immediately snapped it up, knowing it would look just gorgeous filled with a natural, free-form collection of flowers. The rough-hewn clay gives it an aged appearance, as if it might have sat out in a field for years, and this makes it a natural vessel for the wildflowers. (This bouquet would definitely look out of place in a crystal vase.) If you can't find the sort of urn shown here, a large ceramic vessel glazed an earthy brown would be a good substitute.

88

To make the arrangement, place the roses at the outer edge of the container, so that the dark-green rose foliage will disguise the thin, twiglike stems of the wildflowers. I put the wildflowers in the center of the arrangement because of their natural height. Resist the temptation to arrange the flowers in a precise way. Instead, let the natural bend of the grasses, the offshooting stalks of wildflowers, and the groupings of small white flowers mimic the beauty these blossoms have in the field.

89

- *'Toulouse Lautrec' roses*
- *'Jean Giono' roses*
- *Chamomile*
- *Lysimachia*
- *Fern*
- *Lamb's ear*
- *Ribbon*

# MOTHER'S DAY

Yellow garden roses and bright, cheerful chamomile, simply united in this lovely, sensible package, offer the perfect way to communicate love and gratitude to a deserving mother or grandmother. Evocative of a beautiful field in Austria, the arrangement has a rustic look that becomes even more charming when neatly packed into a trim, no-nonsense basket with leather handles for carrying.

Early in my career I heard that yellow roses are symbols of joy and friendship, and ever since then golden-hued blossoms have inspired fond thoughts of my friends and family. Although I later discovered that in the Victorian language of flowers yellow indicated jealousy, I've always embraced my first, more pleasant association with the color—one of the main reasons I chose two yellow Romantica roses as the focal point for this Mother's Day gift. The two roses have subtle differences in color and form. The delicately ruffled, golden-yellow 'Toulouse Lautrec', a Romantica rose, has a distinctive antique appearance, although it was in fact introduced in the United States from France in 1994. The 'Jean Giono', also a Romantica rose, has larger, dahlia-shaped blossoms with variegated color ranging from golden yellow and apricot to hints of tangerine. Chamomile flowers have the look of tiny daisies, and their white petals and green-yellow button centers contrast in size and color with the roses. The lysimachia flower—a white, textured cone that has an elegant bend—adds shape and texture to the display, as do the ferns, which I picked straight from the garden. Lysimachia flowers can be found at flower markets; chamomile is not common in shops, so if you can't find it outside your door, you may have to find a substitute. One option is to use ferns all the way around and punctuate the arrangement with wax flower, which has an appealing combination of thick green leaves and tight clusters of small, waxy white flowers. You can also substitute yellow hothouse roses such as 'Island' or 'Skyline' roses for the 'Toulouse Lautrec' and 'Jean Giono' garden rose. These

90

varieties will lack the strong fragrance and "old rose" shape that gives this display its springtime lushness, but they will provide the needed shot of sunny yellow.

Two buckets transform this basket into a wonderful vessel for flowers. The leather has a wonderful rustic appeal, particularly when tied with textured ribbon that picks up the color of the flowers. The basket should be large enough to contain 2 buckets for the flowers, yet small enough that it appears utterly packed with a profusion of blooms.

The first step is to submerge a block of Oasis (floral foam) in water until it becomes very heavy, approximately 10 minutes. Mash the Oasis with your fingers into pebble-sized nuggets and split the total amount into 2 equal piles; place a pile at the bottom of each bucket. I make 2 arrangements, one for each bucket, and the process is the same. Place the flowers in buckets starting with the lamb's ear as the base and building around it with the roses. Don't worry too much about getting the flowers into the perfect shape on the first try. Using Oasis, it's easy to start over if the shape of the first arrangement doesn't turn out as desired. The oft-repeated rule about placing the tallest flowers at the center of an arrangement is mostly obeyed here: I've placed the chamomile, which has more height than the rest of the flowers, in the middle. The lysimachia is also tall, but its swan's-neck shape doesn't make it an ideal centerpiece. Instead it should be used to adorn the arrangement around its edges, as should the fern. The way I do it is to put the lamb's ear and roses in place, and then add fern and lysimachia wherever it's needed to add flair to the overall shape. The fuzzy green leaves of the lamb's ear create a natural camouflage around the bag's top rim. For the final touch here, I added an Austrian-inspired ribbon that enhances the bright, wild look of the arrangement.

*A Bouquet of Roses*

- *'Dakar' roses*
- *'Yellow Island' roses*
- *Quince*

## Quince and Roses

With its iridescent color and fluted edges, this vintage cake stand sets the stage for a different kind of arrangement. Its remarkable shape and color make it a work of art in its own right and, piled high with gleaming yellow roses and pale green quince, it becomes a magical centerpiece. The raised stand is an ideal platform to showcase the contrasting forms of fruit and flowers.

Creating a seasonal piece is remarkably easy using a platter or cake stand, because such a serving piece offers broad, flat surfaces that are large enough to contain not only flowers but also branches and seasonal fruit. Quince, a relative of the apple and pear, is an excellent choice for autumnal arrangements. It provides an elegant alternative to the folksy orange pumpkins and gourds that make frequent appearances in fall. Your garden or local farmers' market is the best place to find quince as shown here, with its lustrous green leaves and branches still attached. If you can't find quince, pear is a good substitute. The fruit branches have a natural, rustic charm that's perfectly suited to an autumn centerpiece. The quince's yellow green, speckled fruit pairs beautifully with nearly any shade of yellow rose, making this arrangement

very flexible and easy to create no matter what variety of rose you have within reach. I chose two roses with slightly contrasting hues. The full blossoms of the 'Dakar' roses, in the foreground, are deeper gold, while the 'Yellow Island' roses, in the background, are pale buttery yellow. This arrangement of glowing roses and autumnal fruit instantly evokes the rich atmosphere of this bittersweet time of year.

The first step is to arrange the quince and its branches and leaves on one half of the cake stand, making sure that some branches point upward so the arrangement works on several levels and has dimension. As for the roses, I begin with several stems in one hand, and add more until I'm holding a balanced arrangement. In this case, I grouped the 'Dakar' variety together and the 'Yellow Island' variety together,

93

since this creates an accumulation of color that heightens the subtle contrast between the two. Next I place the rose bouquet on its side and tuck the stems beneath some of the quince branches, which should effectively hold them in place. It may take a bit of rearranging to get just the right form, but these minor adjustments are part of the fun. As you put on the final touches, give the container a one-quarter turn every so often. This will help you keep an eye on the balance of the overall display, creating a shape that pleases your eye.

If you don't have a cake stand, one makeshift alternative is to find a bowl with a very flat bottom and—very carefully—balance a plate on top of the upside-down bowl. However, it's worth seeking out cake stands, which can add an element of unexpected shape. Keep in mind that this arrangement may appear washed out if set upon white linen, while it positively glows against dark wood, as shown here.

- *'Jade' roses*
- *Lady slipper orchids*
- *'Gina Lollobrigida' roses*
- *Phalaenopsis orchids*
- *Green spider chrysanthemums*
- *'Skyline' roses*

## SUMMER PALETTE

'Jade' roses inspired this emerald-green palette spiked with yellow and purple. Casual and bright, these small, easy arrangements are ideal for outdoor parties, and they seem especially appropriate in summer when everything from leafy oak trees to lush park lawns turns a bright, vibrant green. Whether the occasion is a summer picnic with friends or a big party in the backyard, these will bring an optic touch to your festivities.

In the simple, bright cupfuls of flowers shown here, roses and orchids come together and capture the exuberance of an outdoor party. It's an especially fun combination because it's a bit unpredictable. Orchids, which have a reputation for being expensive and best suited to sophisticated arrangements, show off their more casual and playful side here. Avid flower arrangers will want to become acquainted with some of the many orchid varieties, since they are available throughout the year and are excellent additions to all sorts of arrangements. Just about every type of orchid will pair wonderfully with roses, and they come in a wide array of colors and interesting shapes. The whimsical green and white striped lady slipper orchids (my personal favorite) give this display its refreshing, unusual look; they remind me of something out of *Alice in Wonderland.* The purple phalaenopsis orchid (background) has a more traditional flower silhouette and is frequently found in shades of vibrant fuchsia or creamy white. The 'Jade' roses are available year-round but generally need to be special ordered; if you have trouble finding them you can go entirely with 'Skyline' yellow roses. The other flowers will provide plenty of contrast, even without the green roses. The 'Gina Lollobrigida' is a French hybrid rose that you will likely need to special order if you don't have any growing in your cutting garden. The 'Madeline' rose is a good substitute that can more often be found in floral shops.

When I'm looking to create festive arrangements for an outdoor occasion, I usually search out bright, fun, and *unbreakable* containers. The iridescent tin cups pictured here are an

inexpensive option, but you could easily use clear glasses instead if that's what you happen to have on hand. The orchids are quite voluminous and a good flower to start with when making the bouquets. I usually place these in the cup first, and then follow by adding the roses. Don't try to make all of the arrangements match—part of the fun here is playing with color and shape to make each cupful of flowers unique. The key is to choose texturally interesting flowers in complementary colors. The mums are a nice touch because their volume camouflages the rims of the cups. It's fun to use a series of containers because you can scatter them or cluster them depending on the occasion. For example, if there's a particular focal point you want to draw attention to, placing clusters of floral arrangements near it will create maximum impact. It's a really versatile approach to flower arranging, perfect for the host or hostess who doesn't do much planning in advance. For an outdoor party, simply follow the theme of the flowers by choosing colorful party decorations and linens. With these easy arrangements, all you have to do is fill the cup with water, cut the stems, and kick back to enjoy summer's simple pleasures.

# Orange
## Originals

# Orange Originals

103

- *'Autumn Gold' roses*
- *'Rio Samba' roses*
- *'Jean Giono' roses*
- *Teddy bear sunflowers*

## SUNSET BOUQUET

Among the colors in nature's palette, the brilliant orange gold hue of sunset is perhaps my favorite because the various tints and shades have a vibrant, layered quality—and each sunset is unique. These glowing roses evoke that moment of extraordinary color. Each type of flower here captures a slightly different shade of orange and gold, and together they mimic the effect of sunset washing over the evening sky.

It's nearly impossible to imagine creating arrangements without yellow and orange roses. Yet these two colors are relatively recent arrivals to the rose world, having become widely available only after hybridization around the turn of the eighteenth century. Ever since their debut, these colors have inspired adoration and devotion. The roses here are wonderful examples of hybrids that display truly spectacular mixtures of color. I'm especially fond of 'Rio Samba', a Hybrid Tea that dates to 1991. The flowers open only moderately, but the rosy golden petals are tipped with a fiery orange that sometimes carries even a slight hint of crimson. This arrangement is a natural fit for outdoor entertaining; its bright colors pop against the rugged setting. It's also remarkably easy to make—the perfect addition to a casual party where you want unfussy flowers that your guests will love.

In an arrangement that is made almost entirely of roses, including blooms in different stages of development provides a sense of movement and texture. The deep-cupped, fully opened flowers contrast with the slightly more furled, pointed blossoms. This tonal arrangement in shades of orange and yellow is easy for the novice, because the flowers will look quite natural in any formation thanks to the overall monochromatic color scheme. Grouping the various shades of roses together, as shown here, is a nice approach because it gives more definition to each layer of color.

A good way to start this bouquet is to hold several stems of the 'Autumn Gold' roses in one hand, and then add 'Rio Samba' and 'Jean Giono' roses until the bouquet is too large to hold; at that point, place it in your container, and add the teddy bear sunflowers in key places.

The sunflowers bring texture to the arrangement and have a voluminous look that effectively
camouflages the rim of the container. I prefer a
glass bowl for this full, lush display because it
mimics the shape of the arrangement—not to
mention the round shape of the setting sun.

- *'King's Pride' roses*
- *Sedum*
- *Green and white lisianthus*
- *Lamb's ear*
- *Grain*

## CANTALOUPE ROSES AND LAMB'S EAR

Hues of apricot, peach, gold, and cream beautifully merge in roses the color of cantaloupe, a shade that is among my most beloved. Their color looks especially lovely with the subtle contrast of the pale green lamb's ear and delicate white lisianthus flowers. For my part, I can imagine no better welcome to a room than this soothing combination of colors, particularly in this vessel, which beckons with silky iridescence.

When I spotted this green iridescent pot at one of my favorite garden stores, I couldn't resist its wonderful luminous quality. After experimenting with several types of flowers, I found that cantaloupe-colored roses create an ideal contrast with its cool, shimmering glaze. Pairing the roses with silvery green lamb's ear further highlights the many tints in the glaze. With its soothing, light colors and small scale, the arrangement is a perfect addition to the bedroom, whether it welcomes a guest or serves as a special treat for yourself. The 'King's Pride' rose has an enormous bloom and a gorgeous color and is readily available throughout the year. In summer, when David Austin garden roses are available, you might substitute 'Abraham Darby' roses, which carry a marvelous scent in addition to a beautiful hue and feature full-cupped blossoms reminiscent of an antique rose.

The first step in creating this type of densely packed arrangement is to choose a voluminous plant base to anchor and control the other flowers. Although hydrangeas are my usual choice, this arrangement called for something less flowery to balance the lushness of the 'King's Pride' roses. The flower I settled on, sedum, has dark-red bristly heads that make a deep, textured background. After placing the two primary flowers—in this case, the sedum and the 'King's Pride' roses—my usual technique is to add three or four more kinds of flowers that round out the arrangement. Here, I chose the silvery green, fuzzy leaves of lamb's ear to provide a color contrast and subtle foil for the stalks of grain,

*A Bouquet of Roses*

creating a natural, organic look. To add a breath
of white, I included some lisianthus buds at the
very last minute. A short, wide-mouthed container is best for this arrangement; if you don't
have a light-colored ceramic pot on hand, a clear
or frosted glass bowl would be a fine alternative.

- *'Abracadabra' roses*
- *'George Burns' roses*


## Orange Color Splash


One glimpse of these striking, multicolored roses banded and speckled with color, and it's easy to imagine an artist splashing each blossom with bright, vivid paint. Look closely, and you find that each of the roses is a tiny work of art. When you put them together in an arrangement, they create a look that is modern, bold, and utterly memorable.

I don't think it pays to be cautious with color, which is why I embarked on an experiment to pair these two bright, different multicolor roses. The result—this arrangement of the speckled burgundy 'Abracadabra' rose with the orange and yellow 'George Burns'—was worth the risk. The 'George Burns' rose, with its variegated yellow, orange, and red flower and citrus perfume, has become very popular since its introduction in 1998. It's a Floribunda rose, a type that blossoms in clusters rather than one per stem, and is often used in landscaping because of its hardiness and disease-resistant qualities. But as the 'George Burns' variety proves, the blossoms of a Floribunda can be just as shapely and striking as any other modern rose. Floribundas, which emerged early in the twentieth century, have a fascinating history. While the origins of some rose families are vague, the introduction of Floribundas is directly attributed to a particular Danish family, the Poulsons, whose mission to create a rose that could withstand their country's cruel winters ended in very successful results. Although no rose has multiplied quite so voraciously as the Hybrid Tea, the Floribunda is definitely a runner-up, with many colorful new varieties emerging each year.

The color of a rose often leads naturally to a particular type of container; for example, with pale pink roses I'm often drawn to ladylike shapes, such as antique silver urns or delicate glasses. The minute I saw these large, bold multicolored roses I pictured them in a confident, architectural arrangement. The unusual fluted sides and interesting angles of this fan-shaped metal container make a statement and balance the vivid blossoms with the vessel's texture and weight. This container looks particularly nice in

109

angled spaces, such as a windowsill or a bookshelf, or in the center of a buffet, complemented by small bowls of citrus fruit. In general, containers in this form—narrow at the bottom with an expanded opening on top—bring the flowers into focus while adding dimension. This type of vessel can be found at a garden center, or even at an antique store that carries garden adornments; stone or cast-iron urns would be a good choice for this arrangement as well.

Making this arrangement couldn't be simpler; the only thing to watch out for is the length of the stems. Since this arrangement consists only of roses, you'll want the stems to be short enough that they bend and drape to camouflage the rim of the container, but also long enough that the blooms really show their heads. One easy little trick is to put the flowers in the container, measuring them against its height, before you clip the stems. After clipping them, I put in the 'George Burns' roses first and then fill the rest of the container with the 'Abracadabra' roses. Make sure that you leave buds on the 'George Burns' for a just-picked look. The true beauty of these fiery blossoms is brought forth when lit from above, or from behind by the sun.

- *'Sari' roses*
- *'Tequila' roses*
- *'Circus' roses*
- *'Abraham Darby' roses*
- *Rose hips*
- *Cone hydrangeas*
- *Burgundy calla lilies*
- *Seckel pears, plums, apples, persimmon branches*

# AUTUMN HARVEST

Bushels of fruit from apple orchards, bright orange pumpkins scattered across the turned fields, a crisp coolness in the air, and tree leaves in every imaginable color of red and gold—these are the signs of the harvest season and also my inspiration for this cornucopia. In this season of holidays and family gatherings, a magnificent autumnal arrangement is always welcome at the table.

Evoking the colors of autumn with a rose arrangement is remarkably easy, thanks to a vast array of blooms that range from hot orange and gold to radiant apricot. To capture the many shades of fall, I used four different roses in various hues. The 'Sari' rose is true orange, the 'Tequila' rose is more subdued with hints of warm brown, and the 'Circus' rose has petals tipped with orange. The 'Circus' rose varies in color and always brings something different to the table; this Floribunda, an All-American Rose Selection in 1956, develops its variable hues of pink and coral with exposure to sunlight. All three of these roses are hothouse varieties that should be readily available from a florist. The wild card in the arrangement is the 'Abraham Darby', a richly scented, apricot-colored David Austin rose. It's still possible to special order this garden rose in early fall, and I wholeheartedly recommend that you do, since no hothouse variety can compete with its beautiful apricot color and strong fragrance. Perhaps even more than fiery colored roses, the bright orange rose hips capture the spirit of autumn. Dangling over the container's rim, they show off the same graceful quality they have in nature, when they colorfully adorn rose bushes that have been stripped of their leaves and flowers by the cold weather. Their distinctive bulb shape also complements autumn fruits such as persimmons and Seckel pears.

III

Elaborate arrangements with a considerable list of elements, like this one, are often viewed as intimidating or expensive to create. Trying your hand at one is the only way to find out that it's actually within reach, even for novice arrangers. As for cost, much of the volume and drama in this arrangement is provided by the more affordable items, such as cone hydrangeas and fruit branches. These items can be found at a produce stand, farmers' market, or, if you're in the country, an orchard. The first step is to find the right container, something that speaks of autumn; in this case, the vessel is an old wooden pot from the garden shed and the platform is a wooden cake stand. Putting the flowers together is quite straightforward. I start by setting the hydrangeas around the outer rim of the container so the fluffy blossoms will help camouflage the rim.

Then I gather the roses in one hand, first grouping the brightest orange, the 'Sari' roses, and then adding in color accents using the brownish orange 'Tequila' rose and the apricot 'Abraham Darby'. When the bouquet is complete, I cut the stems and place it into the middle of the container so it's surrounded by the hydrangeas. Periodically giving the vase a one-quarter turn to achieve a balanced display, I add the burgundy calla lillies and rose hips stem by stem until the arrangement is finished. Scattering the branches and fruit about the cake stand is like playing with blocks—if you don't like the way they look, start over. In no time you'll find the architecture that pleases your eye.

# Lovely
## Lavender

# Lovely Lavender

117

- *'Blue Curiosa' roses*
- *'Heirloom' roses*
- *'Stainless Steel' roses*
- *Lavender hydrangeas*
- *Black calla lilies*

## MAUVε MIX

Whether it's a garden filled with lilacs, a field of lavender, or a handful of velvety violets, nature provides a nearly endless array of tints and shades of purple. A similarly wide range of this rich color exists among roses as well. I play up its many subtle variations in this lush arrangement, which stars several of my favorite lavender roses.

Mauve, lilac, lavender, violet, plum, wine—bringing together multiple shades of purple in a densely packed arrangement creates a lush impression. The key is to select roses in distinctive shades that work well together in a monochromatic color scheme. This arrangement includes three types of roses, each with a different intensity. 'Heirloom' roses, which are Hybrid Teas colored deep purple to lilac, are at the darker end of the color spectrum and have an inviting fragrance and full blossoms. The pale, silvery lavender of the 'Stainless Steel' rose, a Hybrid Tea introduced in 1991, lightens up the display with its large, strongly perfumed flowers. This rose is a descendant of the famous 'Sterling Silver' rose, which electrified the modern rose world when it was introduced in 1957 with its intensely fragrant, ever-blooming blossoms that were truly mauve—a rarity in those days. Now, mauve roses are relatively easy to find, and 'Blue Curiosa' roses are accessible in floral shops throughout the year. That certainly doesn't make them ho-hum; 'Blue Curiosa' are a staple in my floral world. Plush hydrangeas, combined with the appealing Art Deco formality of calla lilies, add a touch of sophistication to this lush rose display. With its many hues of lavender and pleasant rose fragrance, this arrangement brings an appealing touch to any special occasion. It also contrasts beautifully with rustic outdoor textures, making it one of my favorite bouquets for a casual summer party.

It's important to find a vessel large enough to adequately contain the stems, yet small enough to convey the impression that the bowl is brimming over with a profusion of gorgeous flowers. The container can be any sort of bowl, just as long as it's deep enough—in this case, I

118

sought out a lavender bowl of thick glass. To create this arrangement, first place the anchoring hydrangeas in the bowl and then add the roses, one stem at a time. An alternative approach is to hold the stems of hydrangea in one hand, and then add roses until the bouquet is too big to hold. Once the bouquet is assembled, cut all the stems quite short and place the flowers in the container. Finally, add calla lilies for added color contrast and sculptural interest. (This flower tends to drink up a fair amount, so replenish the water in your container frequently.) Callas are so distinctively shaped that some arrangers shy away from placing them with other flowers—but I love the marked contrast they create when set against the more voluptuous shapes of hydrangeas and roses. I group the callas and the

hydrangeas together in one segment of the bouquet rather than sprinkling them around—this prevents them from looking misplaced, making them look instead like a purposeful, dramatic element. The effect focuses the eye, allowing the viewer to take in the color and texture of each flower variety as he or she gazes at the overall display. One flower placed at random by the next does not make as much of a statement in shape and texture as several flowers placed together do. Grouping flowers in this manner creates a wonderful, elegant look and makes the most of their natural beauty.

- *'Heirloom' roses*
- *'Blue Curiosa' roses*
- *Purple basil, opal basil, blooming oregano, blooming mint*

## ROSES BY THE BATH

Nature's ultimate aromatherapy might just be a bouquet of gorgeous lavender-tinted roses and fresh blooming herbs set next to the tub. It's the next best thing to bringing an entire wine-country garden indoors. Add some fresh rose petals to the bath water, light some candles, and the room instantly becomes a heavenly refuge.

The beautiful purple bloom and strong, evocative fragrance of the 'Heirloom' garden rose, a Hybrid Tea, make it an excellent choice for a scented bouquet. If you have trouble finding this variety, it's fine to create the bouquet entirely with 'Blue Curiosa', a lovely lavender rose that's available throughout the year. (It carries more of a rose scent than most other hothouse roses, although it can't compete with the glorious fragrance of the 'Heirloom'.) I encourage you to mix and match the roses with herbs at will, experimenting to find the scent combination that pleases you the most. The best source for blooming herbs is your own backyard, since most floral shops will not carry them, although you may be able to find them at your local farmers' market or garden center. Most herbs are not only beautiful and fragrant but also therapeutic. The herbs in this bouquet have long been used as aids in health and beauty, and some, it is said, have links to the spiritual world. Crushed fresh basil leaves, which emit a slightly sweet, delicate aroma, have been traditionally used in facial steam baths to relieve headaches and colds. Indigenous to India, the basil plant is sacred to Vishnu and is believed to embody his wife, Lakshmi; it's traditionally grown near Hindu temples and homes to freshen the air. Mint is considered restorative, and its strong, refreshing scent is known for warding off exhaustion and nausea. Many herbs in your garden could substitute beautifully for any of those included here, although I'd recommend searching out fragrant specimens that are lavender or purple in color. Options to consider include the ever-popular English lavender; purple sage, an evergreen shrub with textured leaves that flowers in springtime with tiny mauve-blue blossoms; and herbs such as thyme or rosemary in bloom.

As far as I'm concerned, anything goes when it comes to containers, as you might guess, since I've put these flowers in an antique white ironstone chamber pot. I love the texture and thickness of ironstone, and the handle on the pot gives it character. With this arrangement, as with the other low, densely packed displays in the book, the key is to start the arrangement with a voluminous flower base and then add the accent flowers, in this case the blooming herbs. Begin by holding several roses in one hand and inserting other stems through the top with the opposite hand until you are holding a full bouquet. Once the flowers are firmly in place in the container, add the herbs, clustering each type together for maximum fragrance. Floral foam such as Oasis shouldn't be necessary if you use a low, wide vessel similar to this one—even a nice mixing bowl from the kitchen cupboard will do the trick—although foam will help if you find that the flowers are not staying put. It's important to have enough volume so that some of the blossoms naturally lean and bend at the rim to hide its edge. All that remains is to scatter the room with glowing candles, sink into the bath, and relax and enjoy this indulgent aromatherapy treatment.

*A Bouquet of Roses*

- *'Leonidas' roses*
- *'Blue Curiosa' roses*
- *'Stainless Steel' roses*
- *'Heirloom' roses*
- *Ribbon*

## KISSING BALL

In Victorian England, holiday tradition called for kissing balls of festive greenery and bright holly to be hung from doorways or rafters; any two people caught beneath them shared a kiss of friendship or romance. This assembly of beautiful Hybrid Tea roses is a fun, easy way to carry on this tradition in your own home. Incorporating unusual shades of lavender and terra-cotta, this sophisticated incarnation of a kissing ball brings merriment to any occasion and fills the room with fragrant rose perfume.

Equally suited to holiday events and other festive parties, the kissing ball can be made with any color you please. For a traditional Yuletide look, try using red roses, or stick with this elegant and pleasing combination of lavender and terra-cotta blooms. I used four types of roses and arranged them in a subtle, striped pattern. Two of the roses, the 'Leonidas' rose and the 'Blue Curiosa' rose, are hothouse varieties available year-round from your florist, so it's possible to create this kissing ball even during the winter. The lightly fragrant 'Leonidas', a Hybrid Tea that arrived in 1995, boasts a truly unusual and beautiful cinnamon-orange color. Its warm, earthy tint is an ideal contrast for the shimmering lavender blossoms of 'Blue Curiosa', also a Hybrid Tea. In addition, I used two garden roses,

the pale, silver gray lavender 'Stainless Steel' rose and the deeper lilac purple 'Heirloom' rose. Don't fret if you can't find these in December, since the kissing ball can easily be made without the garden roses. Simply replace them with hot-house varieties in similar shades. You could even get away with using only two types of roses (such as the 'Leonidas' and 'Blue Curiosa'). However, it's the four different-colored roses placed together that help make this particular kissing ball so festive and elegant.

The base of this arrangement is an Oasis ball, the green floral foam widely available in floral shops. The first step is to wrap a 3-inch ball of Oasis with 2 pieces of wired ribbon, 18 inches long (you can also use 22-gauge floral wire). Attach the ribbon or wire to the foam with

125

Oasis pins (sold at craft-supply stores). Wrap the ribbon or wire around the ball of Oasis, in the same manner with which you would wrap a gift box. Twist the ends together and curl into a 1-inch loop. Make sure your roses are fully opened, because the full blooms are needed to obscure the ribbon or wire. Soak the foam in water until it becomes heavy and saturated, about 10 minutes. Cut the flowers approximately 2 inches below the bloom (you need about 2 inches of stem). Once the stems are all cut to the same length, insert colored roses in rows around the ball. The ball will be quite heavy when all the flowers are in place; if you have ceiling molding, hang the kissing ball from it to avoid marring your wall with tack or nail holes. For the ribbon handle, tie an 18-inch length of ribbon to the previously mentioned loop. Consider the color of the ribbon you will use for the handle; here, the dark satin ribbon handle lends an elegant effect. Keep in mind that the kissing ball is not a long-lasting piece and is best used to decorate for a special evening such as a holiday party.

Note: This display is technically challenging and probably not a good first project for novice arrangers.

*A Bouquet of Roses*

# Bibliography

Austin, David. *David Austin's English Roses*. Boston: Little, Brown, and Company, 1993.

Blacker, Mary Rose. *Flora Domestica: A History of British Flower Arranging*. New York: Harry N. Abrams, 2000.

Brenzel, Kathleen Norris, ed. *Sunset Western Garden Book*, 7th ed. Menlo Park, Calif.: Sunset Publishing, 2001.

*Language and Sentiment of Flowers and the Classical Floral Legends, The*. London: Frederick Warne and Co., 1883.

Markley, Robert. *Encyclopedia of Roses*. New York: Barron's Educational Series, 1999.

Reddell, Rayford. *The Rose Bible*. San Francisco: Chronicle Books, 1998.

Schneider, Peter, ed. *Taylor's Guide to Roses*. Boston: Houghton Mifflin, 1995.

White, Hazel. *Roses*. Menlo Park, Calif.: Sunset Publishing, 2003.

## INDEX

Pears, 93, 111

Peonies, 50, 53, 59, 81

'Perdita,' 58

Persimmons, 111

Phalaenopsis orchids, 96

'Pilgrim,' 14

Pink
  arrangements, 48–64
  rose varieties, 15

Pink and Green Entryway, 63–64

Pink Classic, 55–56

Plums, 111

Portlands, 12

Poulson family, 109

### Q

Queen Anne's lace, 88

Quince and Roses, 93–95

### R

Red
  arrangements, 28–43
  rose varieties, 15

Reddell, Ray, 17

Ribbon, wired, 21

'Rio Samba,' 88, 104

Roses. *See also individual varieties*
  cutting, 18
  double, 14, 55
  families of, 12
  full, 14, 55

garden vs. hothouse, 12, 13

history of, 11–12

preparing and conditioning, 17–18

purchasing, 13

scent of, 13

varieties of, by color, 14–15

Roses by the Bath, 121–22

### S

'Sahara,' 61, 76

'Sari,' 111–12

Satellite arrangements, 53–54

Scabiosa, 38, 73

'Secret,' 33, 48–49, 50, 55

Sedum, 106

Series arrangements, 39

Simple Rose Bowls, 42–43

'Skyline,' 88, 90, 96

'Stainless Steel,' 118, 125

'Sterling,' 12, 63

'Sterling Silver,' 118

Succulents, 73

Summer Palette, 96–98

Sunflowers, 88, 104–5

Sunset Bouquet, 104–5

'Swan,' 70

### T

Tea and Sympathy, 40–41

Teas, 12

'Tequila,' 111–12

Thorns, removing, 17, 56

'Tiffany,' 55, 82

'Titanic,' 48, 63

'Toulouse Lautrec,' 90

Traditional Bride, 70–72

'Traviata,' 38, 40, 42

Tuberose, 81

Tulips, 53

### V

'Vendela,' 70

### W

Warriner, Bill, 81

White
  arrangements, 70–82
  rose varieties, 15

White Entryway, 81–82

'White Majolika,' 76

Wildflower Celebration, 88–89

### Y

Yellow
  and green arrangements, 88–98
  rose varieties, 15

'Yellow Island,' 93

'Yves Piaget,' 48–49, 55

### Z

Zinnias, 50

*A Bouquet of Roses*